THE VERY BEST OF
TWO FAT LADIES

THE VERY BEST OF TWO FAT LADIES

Over 150 favourite recipes from
their three bestselling books

Jennifer Paterson and
Clarissa Dickson Wright

NOTE: ALL RECIPES SERVE 4 UNLESS OTHERWISE STATED

First published in 1999

Text © Optomen Television and Jennifer Paterson and Clarissa Dickson Wright 1999
Photographs © Ebury Press or Optomen Television 1999
Compilation and introduction © Ebury Press 1999

Recipes first published by Ebury Press in *Two Fat Ladies* (1996), *Two Fat Ladies Ride Again* (1997)
and *Two Fat Ladies Full Throttle* (1998). The recipe on page 65 is reproduced by kind permission
of Grub Street.

Jennifer Paterson and Clarissa Dickson Wright have asserted their right to be identified as the authors
of this work under the Copyright, Designs and Patents Act 1988.

All rights reserved. No part of this publication may be reproduced, stored in a retrieval system, or
transmitted in any form or by any means, electronic, mechanical, photocopying or otherwise without
the prior permission of the copyright owners.

This compilation first published in the United Kingdom in 1999
by BCA by arrangement with Ebury Press
Random House, 20 Vauxhall Bridge Road, London SW1V 2SA

CN 1862

Designed by Alison Shackleton
Jacket design by Jerry Goldie
Food photography by James Murphy and Philip Webb

Printed and bound in Spain by Bookprint, S.L.

CONTENTS

INTRODUCTION

Pat Llewellyn directs the Ladies at the Devil's Bridge at Kirkby
Lonsdale, Cumbria

Since their first series was broadcast by the BBC in 1996 the Two Fat Ladies – Jennifer Paterson and Clarissa Dickson Wright – have become national treasures and international stars. Whether they are chatting to Keanu Reeves in Hollywood or discussing the merits of the Gloucester Old Spot with a pig farmer in the Cotswolds, they are truly global in their appeal.

Their activities have ranged from cooking for the Cambridge First Eight to feeding the nuns of Kylemore Abbey in Co. Galway; catering for a cocktail party at the Brazilian Embassy and providing lunch at a Pony Club gymkhana; they have attended a motorcycle rally and made a Christmas meal for the choirboys of Winchester Cathedral. Between series, they have travelled to America and Australia and seen their books translated into Danish, Dutch and Finnish.

The Very Best of Two Fat Ladies brings you the most popular recipes from their first three books. With years of experience in real kitchens behind them, both can speak with authority and real enjoyment on food and cooking. Their love of the best, freshest and tastiest ingredients is reflected in these recipes, where yoghurt or crème fraîche are rarely acceptable substitutes for cream and many a dish is improved by a slurp of wine or a dollop of butter. These are recipes for real people, with real appetites, so choose your dish and enjoy.

This is the life! Jennifer and Clarissa go punting in Cambridge

Aliens on motorbikes? No, Clarissa and Jennifer dressed up for beekeeping

The ladies receive some direction at Kylemore Abbey in western Ireland, with the Mother Abbess looking on

Move over Carmen Miranda, Jennifer shows how to shake things up behind the bar at the Brazilian Embassy

Relaxing at the end of a long day's filming

SOUPS, STARTERS AND SNACKS

Jennifer and Clarissa prepare to cook

The first course is many people's favourite part of the meal, indeed there was once a highly successful London restaurant that served nothing but starters and puddings. In many ways, the first course is like a TV trail or an advertisement: you want to grab the attention of your guests away from their drinks and their pre-dinner chat and refocus them on to the fact that they are now sitting down to enjoy your food. If you don't do this you will feel like the chef in the Saki story who ran amok and drowned the bandleader in the soup tureen because everyone was listening to the music and ignoring his efforts!

Carry the concept of your whole menu with you at all times. If your main course is light, then you can afford a more robust starter. When we were cooking for the Cambridge University Rowing Eight the main course was a fairly light rabbit dish of mine with a sort of hot salad and so, knowing how hungry they would be, as a starter we gave them a substantial bean soup full of Spanish sausages, ham hocks and other good things (for less hearty appetites this would make a very good main course). The capacity of your guests is another thing to be considered – those glorious golden young men will grow into dilettantes whose ravished palates and sensitive digestions need both titillating and nurturing. Incidentally the oarsmen were so fit that when we were trying to keep pace with them on the

Jennifer demonstrates the importance of having a sharp knife to hand at all times

a mere frivolity. Above all don't lose sight of your menu. Focus on the perspective of the meal when choosing your starter and remember the colours of the dishes and accompaniments in the meal. Nothing is worse than an all white menu, and the different courses should appeal to the eye as well as the stomach.

Clarissa practises what she preaches, shopping for the best ingredients

towpath the bike could barely keep up! It gives a whole different picture to the historic use of water transport to imagine Henry VIII's great gilded barge powered by the likes of those young giants. So much nicer than our dear present Queen's gas-powered taxi!

Some of the best starters are of course the simplest. In cold weather soups are good value, but be careful with cold summer soups – in Scotland, for instance, many people don't seem to like them much and many men think they are

Bahaian Crab Soup

I have always had a fondness for crabs, and where I live I can get live crabs from my beloved fishmonger, David Clark of Fisherrow. The crabs of the Brazilian Atlantic Coast are similar to our own, and in Brazil they use them to make a deliciously spicy soup.

3 good sized crabs or 1kg/2lb crab meat
2 onions, chopped
2 cloves of garlic, finely chopped
2 tbsp olive oil
1 stick of celery, chopped
2 large tomatoes, peeled, deseeded and chopped
1 hot chilli, deseeded and chopped
1 tbsp chopped parsley
2 tbsp chopped fresh coriander plus extra to garnish
1 tbsp chopped fresh basil
1 tin coconut milk
6 limes
salt and freshly ground pepper

Cook your crabs and pick out all the meat. Put the shells in a saucepan, add some of the chopped onion and garlic, and cover with water. Simmer for 20 minutes. Strain and reserve 1.2 litres/2 pints of this stock. (If you are using crab meat, and have no shells, substitute fish stock for the crab shell stock.)

Heat the oil in a heavy saucepan, add the remaining onions and garlic and the celery, and fry for 5 minutes to soften. Add the tomatoes and chilli and cook for another 5 minutes, stirring frequently. Add the parsley, coriander, basil and stock. Bring to the boil and simmer for 15 minutes. Add the crab meat, coconut milk and the juice of 3 of the limes. Season well, then heat through. Serve garnished with a little chopped coriander and slices of lime.

CDW

Fish Soup

This is a simple soup, very suitable for the days in Lent. It has a good flavour and a sufficient feel of penitence about it to please the most rigid of worshippers.

1 large cod's head
1 large onion
1 clove of garlic, chopped
1 stick celery, chopped
1 carrot, chopped
1 tomato, skinned and chopped
1 tbsp olive oil
25g/1oz butter
pinch each of thyme, sage, dill and saffron
1 bayleaf
900ml/1½ pints water
1 tbsp tomato purée
1 tbsp rice
salt and freshly ground pepper
croûtons, to serve

Fry onion, garlic, chopped stick of celery, chopped carrot and tomato in olive oil and butter until the onions are opaque, add the herbs and fry for a little longer. Add the cod's head and bayleaf and water. Bring to the boil and then simmer for about 1 hour. Strain into another saucepan, add the tomato purée and rice and boil for 10 minutes. Add salt and pepper to taste. Fry some croûtons in olive oil and serve with the soup.

JP

Green Fish Soup

This recipe was created by Marion James of the Croque-en-Bouche at Malvern Wells. I am not the first to reproduce it, and indeed I came across it in Lindsay Bareham's wonderful *A Celebration of Soup*. However, I spoke to Marion and she tells me that she has now changed the recipe, to add lemon grass and ginger. I have not tried this and have difficulty in changing the original, as I like it so much.

450g/1lb assorted white fish fillet, skinned and cut in collops (large pieces)
350g/12oz sprouting broccoli or calabrese
25g/1oz butter
1 onion, thinly sliced
1 young leek, thinly sliced
salt and freshly ground pepper
25g/1oz plain flour
1 litre/1¾ pints fish stock flavoured with nutmeg and fennel
150ml/¼ pint double cream

Peel the broccoli stalks, then chop all the broccoli. Cook in a little lightly salted water. Drain, reserving the cooking water.

Melt the butter in a heavy saucepan and soften the onion and the leek, but do not brown. Season with salt and pepper. Add the flour and stir gently for a few minutes. Add a little stock, still stirring. Continue to add all but 150ml/¼ pint of the stock. Simmer for 10 minutes.

Check the seasoning and add the fish. Cook for 1 minute, then set aside to cool slightly.

Transfer to a blender, add the cooked broccoli and process till smooth. Return to the pan, add the cream and reheat gently. The reserved stock and broccoli water can be used to thin the soup if desired.

CDW

Easy Onion Soup with Stilton

This is a very quick and easy onion soup, and a great way of using up left-over wine or beer and post-Christmas Stilton or even Stilton rind. I tend to make this recipe using half wine or beer and half stock, but you can just as easily use all stock and add a glass of wine or beer at the end of cooking. If you don't have any stock use a stock cube.

2 medium onions per person, chopped
25g/1oz butter or 1 tbsp olive oil per person
salt and freshly ground pepper
300ml/½ pint liquid (see above) per person
a pinch of fresh thyme or winter savory
Stilton

In a heavy saucepan heat the fat and sauté the onions. The colour of the finished soup depends on how much you caramelise the onions. I don't like dark brown onion soup, so I cook them to a light gold. It is entirely a matter of personal preference. Season with salt and pepper.

Add the liquid and bring to the boil. Adjust the seasoning and add the thyme. Cover and simmer fiercely for 30–40 minutes.

If you are using Stilton rind, grate it finely. Otherwise, chop the cheese. In either case, add it half way through the cooking and stir well. If adding wine or beer to stock, do so 10 minutes before the end. Serve with croûtons.

CDW

Crème Vichyssoise Glacée

To my mind this is one of the most delicious of iced soups. It was invented in New York in 1917 by Louis Diat, the French chef des cuisines at the Ritz-Carlton. As we can now get leeks all year round this makes a very suitable soup for a lovely summer's day, either at home or taken on a picnic in a sturdy thermos flask.

SERVES 8

6 good-size leeks
55g/2oz unsalted butter
6 medium potatoes, peeled and finely sliced
1.2 litres/2 pints chicken stock or water
salt and freshly ground pepper
175ml/6floz thick cream
fresh chives

Trim the leeks and slice the white parts very finely (you can use the green parts in a fry-up with new potatoes – very good). Melt the butter in a saucepan large enough to contain all the ingredients and stew the leeks until softish. Add the potatoes and stir to mix with the leeks. Pour in the stock or water and season with salt. Bring to the boil, then simmer for 40 minutes.

Allow to cool a little, then whizz the whole lot in a blender until smooth. Leave to get cold, and stir in the cream. Check the seasoning, adding some freshly ground pepper. Chill thoroughly for about 6 hours or overnight. Serve in nice little bowls with snipped chives sprinkled on top.

JP

Beetroot Soup

This is not a real Russian beetroot soup, but a wonderful colour nevertheless. It is quite filling and suitable as a supper dish with very little to follow, or you might like it chilled having removed any fat that rises to the top.

900ml/1½ pints chicken stock
225g/8 oz beetroot, chopped and cleaned
225g/8 oz potatoes, chopped and cleaned
115g/4oz carrots, chopped
115g/4oz parsnips, chopped
55g/2oz celery, fibres removed
1 leek, finely sliced
1 large onion, chopped
1 clove of garlic, finely chopped
55g/2oz goose or chicken fat, or 1 tbsp vegetable oil
1 tsp mixed herbs (*herbes Provençal*)
25g/1oz butter
1 tbsp finely chopped parsley

OPTIONAL:
tomato purée
orange juice
red wine
sherry
soured cream

Bring stock to the boil, add beetroot, potatoes, carrots, parsnips, celery, green leek tops and simmer for about 1 hour. (Beetroot takes a long time to cook!) In the meantime, fry the onions, white part of leek and garlic in the fat or oil in a frying pan until the onions begin to brown, stirring continuously, add the herbs and fry a little longer. Add these ingredients to the saucepan and just bring to the boil. Allow to cool for 5 minutes and add the chopped parsley and then liquidise.

You may enhance the colour of the soup by adding tomato purée – and give flavour by adding either orange juice, red wine or sherry. A swirl of soured cream may be added when serving.

JP

Garbure

This is a French cabbage soup, not unlike the Italian minestrone but without the pasta. A good hearty meal in itself. The goose fat gives an inimitable flavour and can be bought in cans in good grocery stores or delicatessens.

450g/1lb piece of gammon
1.2 litres/2 pints water
1 large potato
1 small swede
1 carrot
1 bouquet garni
1 bayleaf
350g/12oz spring cabbage, shredded
1 large onion, finely chopped
2 cloves of garlic, finely chopped
55g/2oz goose fat or 1 tbsp each of vegetable oil and butter
1 tbsp chopped parsley
pinch of thyme
salt and freshly ground pepper
croûtons, to serve

Put the gammon in a pan, add the water and bring to the boil. Reduce the heat and simmer until the gammon is cooked. Remove gammon and set aside. In the meantime peel the potato, swede and carrot and chop into smallish chunks. Cook these root vegetables in the stock and add the bouquet garni and the bayleaf. Wash the cabbage and shred. Gently fry the onion and garlic in the goose fat, add the pinch of thyme and stir in the onions.

The root vegetables should now be cooked, add the fried onions and garlic to them and then liquidise. Put this soup back in the saucepan, bring to the boil and add the shredded cabbage and cook for a further 10 minutes. Add the chopped parsley. Fry the croûtons in some more of the goose fat or oil and butter. Cut the pieces of gammon into small chunks, place in serving bowls and ladle the soup over. Serve with croûtons.

JP

Asturian Bean and Sausage Soup

My mad wild friends the Herbie boys from the delicatessen of that name in Edinburgh gave me a *mercillo* or Spanish blood sausage, and in return I gave them this recipe. Do not confuse Asturia, which is a Spanish Kingdom, with the land of *lederhosen*. This is a good rib-sticking soup and a meal in itself.

250g/9oz white beans, soaked overnight
200g/7oz ham hock, soaked for 1 hour
140g/5oz belly of pork rib, on the bone
140g/5oz belly of pork, cubed
3 fresh *mercillos* or other or blood pudding
2 or 3 *chorizo* sausages
750g/1½lb dark green cabbage
450g/1lb potatoes
salt and freshly ground black pepper
pinch of paprika, optional

Put all the ingredients except the cabbage and potatoes into a pan and cover with water. Skim as the water comes to the boil and cook for 1 hour or until the beans are almost tender. Cut up the cabbage quite finely and bring to the boil in a saucepan of salted water. Drain. Remove the meat bones returning any shreds of meat to the casserole and slice the sausages. Season with plenty of black pepper and salt to taste. Add the cabbage and potatoes, and more liquid if necessary to cover them comfortably. Simmer until the potatoes are tender and check the seasoning. If your *chorizos* are not very spicy, you could add some paprika. Serve in big bowls with country bread.

CDW

Oeufs en Cocotte (Baked Eggs)

We used to love these as children, probably because we got our own little pots, sometimes covered in grated cheese and put under the grill.

SERVES 6

40g/1½oz butter
6 tbsp double cream
6 large fresh eggs
1 heaped tbsp chopped fresh chives or tarragon
salt and freshly ground black pepper

Use 25g/1oz of the butter to grease 6 cocottes or ramekin dishes. Warm the cream and put a spoonful in each dish. Break an egg carefully into each dish. Sprinkle with salt, pepper and chives or tarragon and dot with the remaining butter. Place the dishes in a large roasting tin and pour hot water into the tin until it comes half way up the dishes. Bake in a preheated oven at 190°C/375°F/Gas 5 for 7–8 minutes. The yolks should still be soft – remember that they will keep on cooking in their little dishes until eaten.

JP

Eggs Benedict

The receipt for this dish originated in America, where it is served on so-called 'English muffins'. It was named for a patron of the Waldorf Astoria Hotel, New York, whose favourite form of eggs it was. These eggs also make a very good luncheon dish.

4 slices of cooked ham
butter
4 slices of white bread
4 eggs
hollandaise sauce

Lightly fry the cooked ham in a buttered frying pan. Toast the bread slices and butter them. Poach the eggs. Put the ham on top of the toast and the poached eggs on the ham, and spoon over some warm hollandaise sauce. Serve straight away.

JP

Welsh Rarebit Soufflés

I think nearly everybody enjoys cheese dishes. This is a variation on the original Welsh rarebit which was in fact pure toasted cheese cooked in the oven. It makes a very good supper dish, or when cut into small pieces, an excellent morsel to go with drinks.

225g/8oz really good mature Cheddar cheese, grated
4 eggs, separated
dry English mustard
Worcestershire sauce
Tabasco
salt and freshly ground pepper
2 large slices of good white bread

Place the cheese in a bowl, beat in 3 egg yolks (use the fourth one in something else), a level teaspoon of mustard, a good shake of Worcestershire sauce and Tabasco, and season to taste. Toast the bread. Whip the 4 egg whites until they stand in stiff peaks. Add a spoonful or so to the cheese mixture then gently fold the rest of them into the bowl. Put the toasts into an ovenproof dish and pour the mixture over them. Bake in a preheated oven at 230°C/450°F/Gas 8 for 10 minutes until browned and risen. Serve at once with a salad or spinach on the side.

JP

Rabbit Pâté

For all that is talked about lean meat, rabbit is still scorned and the wastage of this good and healthy meat every year is immense. I like a delicate rabbit pâté much better than a chicken one, the flavour is real and it is a lot safer.

900g/2lb raw rabbit meat
900g/2lb pork
450g/1lb fat bacon
2 onions, peeled
1 tbsp parsley, finely chopped
2 tsp thyme
3 liqueur glasses brandy
salt and freshly ground pepper
bottle of cornichons (small gherkins)
1 bayleaf
225g/8oz thin rashers of streaky bacon

Coarsely mince or process the rabbit, pork, bacon and onions together, add the other ingredients (except the bayleaf and bacon) and mix, using your hands, until they are all well amalgamated. Half fill an earthenware terrine with the rabbit mixture, then put in a double layer of cornichons. Fill to the top with more mixture, place the bayleaf on top, cover with bacon rashers cut into thin strips and press down well. Add a layer of greaseproof paper. Cover and cook in a bain marie in a preheated slow oven at 150˚C/300˚F/Gas 2 for 1 hour for small terrines, 2 hours if large. To store, pour over a layer of melted lard and cover with a piece of waxed paper. Store in a cool place for a month or more.

CDW

Rabbit and Beer Terrine

Owing to the sentimentalisation of rabbits in the media, tons of this good and by anyone's standards healthy meat is dumped each year. Rabbit is excellent eating and this pleasant terrine makes a fine starter or perfect picnic material.

1kg/2lb boned rabbit
450g/1lb belly of pork, boned and skinned
300ml/½ pint beer
1 bayleaf
fresh thyme and parsley
salt and freshly ground pepper
225g/8oz thin rashers of streaky bacon

Marinate the rabbit and pork in the beer, herbs and seasoning overnight. Drain, reserving the marinade. Mince the meats separately. Line a terrine with the bacon rashers. Layer the meat in the terrine in alternate layers. Pour in the marinade. Cover tightly and bake in a preheated oven at 150°C/300°F/Gas 2 for 2½–3 hours. Keep for a day or two to mature before serving.

CDW

Warm Chicken Liver Salad

I think warm salads are extremely good. The hot sauce gives a great taste to the salad leaves, one of which should be rocket. Rocket's name derives from the Latin word *eruca* which means caterpillar and which was applied to the plant because of its hairy stem. Fancy! Make sure your salad leaves are fresh and crisp.

225g/8oz chicken livers
300ml/½ pint white wine
10 peppercorns
1 clove of garlic, crushed
1 bayleaf
mixed salad leaves
1 tbsp olive oil
4 tbsp balsamic vinegar
3 tbsp double cream

Pat the chicken livers dry and cut away any discoloured or stringy bits. Marinate the livers overnight in a mixture of the white wine, peppercorns, crushed garlic and bayleaf.

Wash the salad leaves and divide among four plates. Dry the chicken livers (reserve the marinade) and cut into bite-size pieces. Heat the olive oil and fry the chicken livers for about 3 minutes, turning occasionally. Remove the livers from the pan and keep warm. Add the balsamic vinegar to the pan and boil, stirring, until the vinegar is reduced by half. Add 3 tbsp of the marinade liquid and cook for another minute or two. Remove the pan from the heat and stir in the cream. Arrange the livers on the salad leaves and pour the sauce over.

JP

Salmon Terrine

A salmon terrine is always a good thing to have up your sleeve in case unexpected guests arrive, especially on a Sunday after cocktails. Easy to make, it can be left in the refrigerator ready to pounce on when necessary.

750g/1½ lb raw salmon, boned and skinned
2 tbsp chopped shallot
4 tbsp dry white wine
225g/½lb whiting or any white fish, boned and skinned
150g/6oz breadcrumbs, soaked in milk and squeezed dry
85g/3oz butter, softened
1 tbsp chopped parsley
2 tsp chopped and blanched chives
¼ tsp nutmeg
salt and freshly ground pepper
1 whole egg and 2 egg yolks, beaten

Cut 450g/1lb of salmon into finger-size pieces and place in a glass dish. Sprinkle with the shallot, salt and pepper to taste and white wine. Place the rest of the salmon, the white fish and breadcrumbs in a food processor and blend together. Add 55g/2oz of butter, parsley, chives and nutmeg and bind the whole lot together with the beaten eggs.

Butter a terrine dish with the remaining butter, put a layer of the forcemeat on the bottom, cover with a layer of salmon fingers, add forcemeat and continue in this fashion until the ingredients are finished. Strain the marinade on to the terrine, put the lid on the terrine and cook in a bain marie in a preheated slow oven at 160°C/325°F/Gas 3 for 1½–2 hours. Leave to get cold.

JP

Potted Shrimps

I am extremely fond of a good potted shrimp, which is becoming more and more difficult to find. As often as not it turns out to be a potted prawn, which is not the same thing at all. They must be those tiny little brown creatures, so if you ever find them south of Morecambe seize and pot them. They will keep well and can, of course, be frozen.

450g/1lb shrimps
(peeled weight)
225g/8oz butter
1 bayleaf
a mustard spoon of freshly
grated nutmeg or mace
freshly ground black pepper
sea salt
cayenne pepper

If the shrimps are frozen, defrost slowly and completely, draining and drying off with paper towels. To clarify the butter, put it in a small saucepan and heat slowly to boiling point. Let it bubble for a few seconds, then strain through a small sieve lined with butter muslin, into a bowl. Leave it to cool and then chill until set.

Tip the butter out of the bowl and scrape off any sediment clinging to the bottom. Put the butter in a bowl set over simmering water. Add the bayleaf, nutmeg or mace, and black pepper and salt to taste. When melted add the shrimps and gently mix everything together. Leave over the heat for 10 minutes, stirring occasionally. Discard the bayleaf, and spoon the shrimps into a straight-sided dish or individual ramekins. They should be just covered by the butter. Leave to cool, then chill in the refrigerator.

Serve, sprinkled with cayenne pepper, as a first course with warm brown toast and butter and lemon wedges. The shrimps will keep 2–3 days in the refrigerator, or 2 weeks if totally sealed with more clarified butter.

JP

Prawns on Sugarcane Sticks

I don't know whether the poor unfortunates in the rest of the United Kingdom can buy sugarcane sticks, but in Edinburgh we can, as we are blessed with the best Mexican/South American deli this side of the pond. It is called Lupe Pintos and is owned by a splendid man named Duggie Bell, who is so wonderfully eccentric that for my first year in Edinburgh I thought 'Lupe' was his nickname. If you can't get sugarcane sticks use wooden saté sticks, but don't forget to soak them first.

olive oil
a 5cm/2in piece of fresh ginger root, chopped
2 cloves of garlic,
2 spring onions, chopped
1 hot chilli, chopped
soya sauce
juice of 2 limes
16 raw tiger or king
4 sugarcane sticks

In a heavy pan heat a little oil and fry the ginger, garlic, spring onions and chilli. Add a dash of soya sauce and the lime juice. Transfer this mixture to a bowl. Add the prawns, turn to coat and leave to marinate overnight.

Thread the prawns on to the sugarcane sticks. Place under a pre-heated hot grill and cook for 3–4 minutes on each side, painting with more marinade once or twice. They can also be cooked on the barbecue. The sugarcane sticks add a wonderful flavour.

CDW

Crab Pâté

A really good fresh crab, with its magnificent claws, always brings joy to my heart. In fact, I think they are even more delectable than lobsters which can often be rather tough, though a perfect one is sublime – straight from the pot to the table. The following recipe will make crab go a lot further than just tucking in with mayonnaise, besides being very delicious with a fine, strong gutsy flavour.

450g/1lb crab meat
(half white meat, half brown)
175g/6oz unsalted butter
4 egg yolks (size 1 or 2)
4 tbsp double cream
3 tbsp medium sherry
4 tbsp freshly grated Parmesan
Tabasco sauce
lemon juice

Melt the butter in a saucepan big enough to receive the rest of the ingredients. Stir in the crab meat, both colours (you can even use the frozen packs at a pinch; they come in 225g/8oz packs). Heat gently, stirring all together. Beat the egg yolks, cream and sherry together, then pour into the crab mixture. Continue to cook and stir until it all thickens. Keep the heat low, we don't want any crumbling. Add the cheese and melt. Take off the heat and season with Tabasco and lemon juice to taste. Allow to cool.

Give the mixture a final good stirring, then pour into a soufflé dish and chill for 6 hours or overnight. Eat with hot brown toast and butter, though it hardly needs it.

JP

Smoked Trout, Avocado and Shrimp Mousse

This is a very 1960s type of mousse, when the thrill of the avocado had just about reached us. However, it is always very good and I like to eat it with hot brown toast and a squeeze of lemon on the side.

2 fillets (225–275g/8–10oz) smoked trout
1 ripe avocado
300ml/1 pint crème fraîche
juice of ½ a lemon
2 tbsp finely grated lemon rind
150g/6oz cooked and shelled shrimps
salt and freshly ground black pepper

Skin and bone the trout, peel and stone the avocado and liquidise. Blend with crème fraîche, lemon juice, lemon rind, salt and pepper. Place half the mixture in a ramekin dish, cover with a layer of shrimps and then with the remaining mixture. Chill the mousse well before serving.

JP

Illustrated overleaf

Aberdeen Nips

My grandmother, who was from Aberdeen, firmly believed that one could never have enough smoked haddock. This little dish is an excellent way of using up left-over cooked smoked haddock and is brilliant for drinks parties, for high tea or a snack any time.

350g/12oz cooked smoked haddock
4 egg yolks
300ml/½ pint thick white sauce
salt and freshly ground pepper
cayenne pepper
8 slices of buttered toast, crusts removed, each cut into quarters
paprika

Flake the fish finely. Mix the fish and the egg yolks into the sauce and season with salt, pepper and cayenne pepper. Heat the mixture through gently. Pile on the squares of buttered toast, sprinkle with paprika and serve.

CDW

Acaraje

I had my first ever food experience in Brazil, aged five. When I returned to school, the nuns enquired what I had liked best – the humming birds?, the Christ of the Andes? My reply was: the black beans, braised beef and rice. I have since visited South America several times, but my stomach still gladdens most at the thought of Brazil.

These little bean fritters with dried shrimps are a traditional dish, very moreish and good for parties. If you can get it, the oil for frying should be one-quarter dende oil for the right flavour. This is palm oil and can be bought in Afro Caribbean shops. I serve the fritters with a hot sauce, but it is traditional to serve vatapa with them.

MAKES 20

450g/1lb dried black-eyed beans
1 onion, roughly chopped
1 maleguata chilli pepper or use ½ tsp Tabasco sauce
salt and freshly ground pepper
oil for deep frying
20 small dried shrimps (these can be bought in Asian shops)

Soak the beans overnight in cold water, changing the water once. Then rub the beans between the palms of your hands to free the outer skins, which should float to the surface. Scoop off the skins and discard. Drain the beans. Purée the beans and onion in a food processor. Season with the chilli or Tabasco sauce, salt and pepper. Using two soup spoons, form the bean mixture into small egg shapes. Press a dried shrimp into the centre of each one, and press the bean mixture round to secure it. The shrimp should still stand proud. Heat oil to 180°C/350°F, and fry the fritters in small batches until golden brown all over. Remove with a slotted spoon and drain on kitchen paper. Keep warm in a low oven until they are all fried.

CDW

Meat Patties in Horseradish Sauce

I was surprised when I saw fresh horseradish on sale in Safeway – well done to them. I grow a lot of horseradish but always in a bucket or it takes over, just like mint. Grate the root in a food processor and you won't weep for days. The Scandinavians make much use of it, and this is a Swedish recipe. The Swedes are also fond of pickled beetroot but like it in a sweet pickle, not our harsh vinegar-based one.

2 medium onions, finely chopped
1 tbsp butter
450g/1lb steak, minced
1 medium potato, boiled and mashed
225g/8oz sweet pickled beetroot, grated
1 egg, beaten
3 tbsp milk
1 tbsp capers, finely chopped
salt and freshly ground pepper
oil for frying

FOR THE SAUCE:
300ml/10fl oz cream
salt
cayenne pepper
1 tbsp freshly grated horseradish

Fry the chopped onions in butter until soft and lightly browned. Mix them with the beef, potato, beetroot, egg, milk, capers and seasoning until well combined. Shape into 12 patties and refrigerate for 1 hour. Combine the sauce ingredients.

Heat the oil in a large heavy pan and fry the patties for 5–10 minutes until they are cooked to your liking. I like to drain off any excess oil from the pan and pour it over the patties to heat them through before serving. In Sweden the sauce is served on the side of the plate.

CDW

Sushi

Sushi requires a deft hand. In fact, real sushi makers are trained for years, but you can master a resemblance of the real thing after a few tries.

80g/1lb 1oz sushi rice (short-grain pudding rice is not a suitable alternative)
1 tbsp caster sugar
4½ tbsp rice vinegar or, if unavailable, cider vinegar may be used
1 heaped tsp salt
5 sheets of nori (toasted paper-thin sheets of laver seaweed)

SUGGESTED FILLINGS:
tuna, very fresh or tinned, and shredded lettuce
pickled herring and shredded lettuce
crab sticks with cress
asparagus and mayonnaise
very thin omelette strips with cress
cucumber sticks with cress
avocado with cress and mayonnaise (although not authentic, this is delicious and very popular in America)

Put the rice in a large saucepan with 600ml/1 pint of cold water and allow to stand for 30 minutes. Bring contents of saucepan to the boil and allow to boil rapidly for 1 minute, then cover saucepan tightly and simmer contents for 20 minutes. Remove from the heat and allow to stand for a further ten minutes without removing the lid.

In the meantime, dissolve the sugar in the rice vinegar. Add the salt. Turn the rice into a large bowl and sprinkle over the vinegar mixture to cool the rice quickly and make it shiny.

To make the sushi rolls, place your sushi mat on the table in front of you and put a sheet of nori on top, positioning it about 1cm/½in above the bottom of the mat. Put a thin layer of vinegared rice over the bottom two thirds of the sheet of nori, making sure you spread the rice to the edges. Dipping your spatula in a tumbler of rice vinegar mixed with water will help to spread the rice and prevent stickiness. Place your chosen filling in a thin layer on the rice, just below the centre. Then, pinching the mat and the nori between your fingers at the outer edges, roll the mat over the rice and press gently with your hands. Let the mat fall back, and roll the nori over completely like a swiss roll. Press again lightly with your hands. Place the roll on a plate while you continue to make further rolls. The rolls should be allowed to rest for 2–3 minutes before cutting across into pieces about 1cm/½in thick (use a sharp knife dipped frequently into the vinegar and water mixture to prevent sticking).

If liked, serve sushi with a dipping sauce made from soya sauce mixed with a tiny blob of wasabi (Japanese horseradish) paste.

JP

Squid Tempura

This method of dealing with squid ensures that it is tender. Squid is tough only when over cooked.

675g/1½lb squid (body only),
cleaned
oil for deep frying
lemon quarters
salt

FOR THE BATTER:
2 large egg yolks
450ml/¾ pint iced water
225g/8oz plain flour

FOR THE DIPPING SAUCE:
250ml/8floz stock or water
4 tbsp soya sauce
4 tbsp mirin

Cut the squid bodies into rings, and reserve.

Unlike most batters, the one for tempura should be made immediately before using. Put the egg yolks in a bowl and beat lightly. Add the iced water and again beat lightly. Add the flour all at once and stir briefly, just enough to combine. Do not worry if the batter is slightly lumpy.

Dredge the squid pieces in the batter, shake off excess and deep fry in very hot oil for 1–2 minutes or until golden brown all over. Remove from the oil and drain on kitchen paper. Do not cook too many pieces of squid at once, and don't let the oil temperature drop too much or the batter will be greasy and soggy. The squid is served on individual plates with lemon wedges, plenty of salt and the dipping sauce.

For the dipping sauce, heat the ingredients in a saucepan to boiling point, then reduce the heat to keep the sauce warm until ready to serve. A little grated fresh ginger root and grated Japanese radish (daikon) may be added to the sauce.

JP

Illustrated overleaf

Kipper Rarebit

Our beloved director, Patricia Llewellyn, is, as you might guess, Welsh, and I have in the last year been more kindly disposed towards the Welsh than ever before. So when I decided to resolve to my own satisfaction the rabbit/rarebit debate that has been raging since the eighteenth century, I turned to Welsh history for guidance. The Welsh have always had a passion for cheese, and *caws pobi*, or cheese rabbit, was credited to them in the fourteenth century. Rarebit, meaning soft, seems to come on the scene much later. This dish is, of course, post-1865, as kippers didn't exist before that date.

2 pairs of kippers
600ml/1 pint milk
2 cloves of garlic, crushed
55g/2oz butter
55g/2oz plain flour
115g/4oz strong cheddar or *Penty Bont* cheese, grated
2 hard-boiled eggs, chopped
paprika
8 slices of fried bread or toast, crusts removed, each cut into quarters

Put the kippers in the milk and bring to the boil, then remove from the heat and leave to stand for 5 minutes. Remove the kippers, and take the flesh from the skin and bones. Return the skin and bones to the milk, add the garlic and simmer for 10 minutes; strain. Make a white sauce with the milk, butter and flour. Fold in the cheese and the flaked kipper flesh. Heat through, then add the eggs and paprika to taste. Serve on the fried bread or toast.

CDW

Crab, Corn and Coriander Fritters

This Indonesian dish is so good that you need to allow about a third for the 'Knaves of Hearts' that pass the table as they are being made. The quantities here will make about 45 5cm/2in fritters.

85g/3oz crab meat
6 ears of fresh sweetcorn
1 medium onion, grated
2 tbsp chopped fresh coriander
1 tsp ground coriander
2 cloves of garlic, crushed
3 eggs, lightly beaten
40g/1½oz plain flour
salt and freshly ground pepper
groundnut oil

Cut the sweetcorn kernels from the cob with a sharp knife. Mix together all the ingredients, except the oil. Cover and refrigerate for at least half a day.

Heat a spoonful of oil in a frying pan and drop in tablespoons of the crab and sweetcorn batter. Fry briskly till brown, then turn and cook the other side. A splatter lid is useful as the kernels may burst whilst cooking. Drain the fritters on paper towel and keep warm until all are cooked. Serve as soon as possible.

CDW

Spare Ribs

If you want the rib meat to be really tender you can pre-boil the ribs for 20 minutes before putting them in the marinade. It makes eating them easier, although they are nice messy things to gnaw in the fingers. Provide finger bowls or damp cloths so people can wipe their hands.

2 tbsp oil
3 tbsp clear honey
1cm/½in piece of fresh root ginger, finely chopped
2 tbsp dark soya sauce
2 tbsp hoisin sauce
1 tsp five spice powder
2 cloves of garlic, crushed
900g/2lb spare ribs

Combine all the ingredients, except the spare ribs, in a jug and mix well. Pour over the ribs and leave to marinate for as long as possible, ideally overnight. Place the ribs on a rack in a roasting tin. Cook in a preheated oven at 200°C/400°F/Gas 6 for about 45 minutes, turning the ribs over half way through the cooking time. Allow to cool and serve cold.

JP

Red Peppers Stuffed with Aubergine Purée

Aubergine, eggplant and melanzane are all the same vegetable in different languages, and a favourite of mine. It can be used in so many ways, from delicious fritters to poor man's caviar. These red peppers stuffed with purée give you a double whammy and really are the full monty.

3 medium-sized aubergines
3 tbsp olive oil
1 large clove of garlic, finely chopped
juice of a large lemon
3 tbsp chopped parsley
salt and freshly ground black pepper
4 large red peppers

Make the aubergine purée by grilling the aubergines until the skins are charred and starting to blister which should mean that the pulp inside is soft. Leave to cool slightly then remove the skin by rubbing gently under cold water. Liquidise with the olive oil and then blend in the garlic, lemon juice, 2 tablespoons parsley, salt and pepper. Pour the purée into a bowl.

Cut the peppers in half, remove the stalk and seeds, brush the inside with the remaining olive oil and bake in a moderate oven 180°C/350°F/Gas 4 for about 30 minutes. A quarter of an hour before serving, fill the pepper halves with the aubergine purée, replace in the oven to warm through. After 15 minutes remove the peppers from the oven, sprinkle with remaining parsley and serve with plain toasted bread fingers.

JP

Devilled Kidneys

Devilled kidneys were very popular in Victorian days, but seem to have suffered a decline in more recent times. Lamb's kidneys, being milder than ox or pig's kidneys, are favoured for this dish. Use a light hand when cooking kidneys – over cooked they become nasty, like little bits of leather.

2 tsp Worcestershire sauce
2 tsp mushroom ketchup
1 level tsp English mustard powder
55g/2oz butter, melted
pinch of cayenne pepper
salt and freshly ground pepper
8 lamb's kidneys
1 tbsp vegetable oil
1 desertspoon chopped parsley
lemon wedges

Mix together the Worcestershire sauce, mushroom ketchup, mustard, 25g/1oz of the melted butter, the cayenne pepper, and a seasoning of salt and pepper. Clean the kidneys by removing the outer skin and cutting away the core. Cut each kidney into three or four pieces. Heat the remaining butter with the oil in a frying pan and cook the kidneys for 4–5 minutes, turning occasionally. Pour the sauce mixture over the kidneys and stir for 1–2 minutes to coat the kidneys.

Serve on warmed plates, sprinkled with a little parsley and accompanied by lemon wedges and hot buttered toast.

JP

Sardinian Artichoke Pie

Globe artichokes are very Elizabethan. I know they don't grow too well over here, so snap them up when you see them. Out of season, they are good in jars and any delicatessen worth its salt should have them. This makes a good vegetarian main course as well as an excellent supper dish or starter.

28 artichoke hearts or 12 baby artichokes
150g/6oz white breadcrumbs
225g/8oz grated Parmesan cheese
225g/8oz grated Romano cheese
3 tbsp capers, drained and chopped
3 tbsp olive oil
225g/8oz black olives, stoned and halved
5 medium tomatoes, peeled and thinly sliced
or 1 large tin plum tomatoes, drained and chopped
275g/10oz Fontina or Gruyère thinly sliced

If using whole baby artichokes, trim the leaves, boil until tender and slice thinly. Butter a 25cm/10in spring cake tin and coat with one third of the breadcrumbs. In a bowl mix the Parmesan, Romano and remaining breadcrumbs. Arrange layers in the cake tin beginning with the artichokes, following with capers and olives, tomatoes, Fontina and then the breadcrumb mixture. Drizzle 1 tablespoon olive oil over this and repeat, pressing down well. This should make three layers. Bake in a preheated oven 180°C/350°F/Gas 4 for 25 minutes. Leave to cool for 10 minutes, unmould and serve with salad.

CDW

Onion Tartlets with Anchovies

These are scrumptious little tarts. Eat while still hot, when they just melt in the mouth.

MAKES 20–24

55g/2oz butter
2 large onions, thinly sliced
175g/6oz shortcrust pastry
2 eggs
150ml/¼ pint double cream
salt and freshly ground pepper
20-24 tinned anchovy fillets
a little freshly grated nutmeg

Melt the butter in a saucepan or frying pan and add the onions. Cover and cook over a low heat until the onions are soft and translucent, stirring occasionally to make sure they don't stick and brown. This will take about 30 minutes.

Meanwhile, roll out the pastry and line the 5.5cm/2¼in greased tartlet tins. Beat the eggs and cream together and season generously with the salt, pepper and nutmeg. Add the onions and mix well, then divide the mixture among the tartlet cases. Bake in a preheated oven at 190°C/375°F/Gas 5 for 25–30 minutes. Five minutes before they are ready split the anchovy fillets in half lengthways and place the two halves in a cross on top of each of the tartlets.

JP

Poor Man's Caviar

Serve this as a first course with hot brown toast and a few slices of thinly cut tomato. Caviar it ain't but it is extremely delicious, and of course a lot cheaper.

2 large aubergines
2 tbsp lemon juice
4 tbsp olive oil
salt and freshly ground pepper
paprika
1 large onion, finely chopped
or grated

When buying aubergines make sure they are firm, unbruised and shiny, and not from Holland. Put them on a baking tray and cook in a preheated oven at 220°C/425°F/Gas 7 until they are really soft, about 45 minutes. Pierce with a skewer to make sure. When cool enough to handle, peel them. Mash the flesh in a bowl or food processor until you have produced a totally smooth paste. Mix in the lemon juice and the olive oil. Season to taste with salt, pepper and about ½ tsp paprika depending on whether you are using the hot or the sweet variety. Combine thoroughly with the onion. Place in a nice earthenware bowl, cover with cling film (to avoid stinking out the refrigerator with onion) and chill until very cold.

JP

Blinys

Oh how I love blinys (which are also spelled blinis). When I was a child we had some Russian friends who used to eat them in huge quantities throughout the week before Lent. When we would go to their house, there would be these delicious little pancakes which you could heap with sour cream and caviar, or with cod's roe mixed with cream cheese, crisp bacon fried with spring onion, herrings of all types, chopped liver, smoked sturgeon and all manner of other good things. The Russians also eat them with fruit purée or jam, but I am a savoury bliny addict.

The pancakes are yeasted and made with a mixture of plain flour and buckwheat flour, which gives them a nutty flavour and more texture than an ordinary pancake. My friend Isobel Rutherford has a set of tiny cast-iron bliny pans which I greatly covet, but you can make them successfully in an ordinary small frying pan.

15g/½oz fresh yeast or use 7g/¼oz dried yeast
300ml/½ pint milk, warmed
2 large eggs, separated
150ml/¼ pint sour cream or use 25g/1oz butter or 2 tbsp plain yogurt
1 tsp salt
115g/4oz strong white flour
115g/4oz buckwheat flour
oil for frying

Cream the yeast with a little of the milk, then add the remaining milk, the egg yolks and sour cream. (If you are using ordinary dried yeast, mix it with a little cold water and leave it for 10 minutes before using; easy-blend dried yeast can be added to the flour.) Sift the flour and salt into a bowl and add the yeast mixture. Stir to make a thick batter. Leave for at least an hour in a warm place, or overnight if more convenient. The batter should now look bubbly. Stir it well. Just before cooking, whisk the egg whites until stiff and fold them into the batter.

Heat a little oil in your pan and pour off any excess. Then pour in a tablespoon of the batter. Turn the pancake over when it shows bubbles on the top side. Cook lots – one bliny is never enough!

CDW

Stuffed Tomatoes

This is a very good way of stuffing tomatoes, but do try and get some with a really good flavour — difficult but possible.

8 large tomatoes
225g/8oz minced meat (pork or veal)
a knob of butter
4 slices of hard toast, crumbled
1–2 eggs, beaten
3 tbsp chopped parsley
1 clove of garlic, chopped
freshly grated nutmeg
salt and freshly ground pepper
oil

Cut the top off each tomato, scoop the pulp and seeds out and turn the tomatoes upside down on kitchen paper in order to get rid of all excess liquid. Leave to drain for half an hour.

Fry the meat with the butter in a frying pan until the meat is browned and crumbly. Remove from the heat. Add the toast crumbs, beaten eggs, parsley, garlic, and nutmeg, salt and pepper to taste.

Stuff the tomatoes with the meat mixture and put the tomato lids back on each tomato. Place the tomatoes in a deep ovenproof dish and put a drop of oil on each lid. Bake in a preheated oven at 180°C/350°F/Gas 4 for 30 minutes.

JP

Tomato Summer Pudding

I thought this up while daydreaming over that splendid Italian peasant dish Panzanella. It is essential that you find really good, sweet tomatoes – none of those tasteless Dutch numbers. Passata is a purée of tomatoes, easily found in most supermarkets or delicatessens.

fresh plum or vine tomatoes –
they must have a good taste
salt and freshly ground black
pepper
sugar
tomato passata
lemon juice
Worcestershire and Tabasco
sauces
good stale Italian bread,
decrusted and sliced
a quantity of garlic cloves
virgin olive oil
a large bunch of fresh basil

Have enough tomatoes to overfill the pudding basin you will use. Dip into boiling water and peel them. Chop roughly and sprinkle with good sea salt and black pepper plus a tiny bit of sugar. Pour some passata into a large soup plate and season with lemon juice and Worcestershire sauce, and maybe a touch of Tabasco. Soak the bread slices briefly in this mixture and line your bowl with them, leaving no cracks nor crannies.

To the tomatoes add as much crushed garlic as you fancy, a good measure of olive oil and lots of torn up basil leaves. Adjust the seasoning and pour the whole lot into the bread-lined bowl. Seal the top with more soaked bread. Place a receptacle on top with weights and leave overnight in the refrigerator. Turn out on to a fine dish and surround with goodies – quail's eggs, olives, peppers, capers or what you will. A bowl of sour cream might be passed round with it, or good home-made mayonnaise.

JP

Amish Onion Cake

How strange it must be to be an Amish living the life of a farmer of the 1830s amidst that modernised version of the Roman Empire that is present-day America. One can see the German origins of the Amish in this onion cake with its sour cream and poppy seeds.

3–4 medium onions, chopped
450g/1lb unsalted butter
1 tbsp poppy seeds
1½ tsp each paprika, salt and freshly ground pepper
450g/1lb plain flour
55g/2oz cornflour
1 tbsp white sugar
1 tbsp baking powder
5 eggs
175ml/6floz each milk and sour cream
1 tbsp dark soft brown sugar

Cook the onions gently in 115g/4oz of the butter for about 10 minutes. Stir in the poppy seeds, paprika, salt and pepper and continue to cook until the onions are golden brown. Set aside.

Mix together the plain flour and cornflour, white sugar and baking powder in a bowl. Add 280g/10oz of the remaining butter and rub in to make soft crumbs (this can be done in a food processor). Add 3 of the eggs, one at a time, mixing in well, then add the milk to form a sticky dough.

Beat the last 2 eggs with the rest of the butter. Whip in the sour cream and the brown sugar.

Grease a 25cm/10in round cake tin. Spread the dough on the bottom. Cover with the onion mixture and the sour cream mixture. Bake in a preheated oven at 180°C/350°F/Gas 4 oven for 20–25 minutes. Cool slightly, and serve in wedges.

CDW

Mushroom Pasties

This is a medieval recipe from Maggie Black's excellent *The Medieval Cookbook* which she produced for the British Museum Press. I first served these patties at a lunch which I did for dear Michael Bateman and the *Independent on Sunday* where they had great acclaim. They are excellent for drinks parties or a buffet.

FOR THE PASTRY:
280g/10oz plain flour
½ tsp salt
85g/3oz butter
85g/3oz lard

FOR THE FILLING:
450g/1lb mushrooms (Paris mushrooms are best)
2 tbsp olive oil
salt and freshly ground black pepper
55g/2oz Cheddar cheese, grated
¼ tsp dry mustard
1 egg, beaten

To make the pastry cases, sift the flour into a bowl and rub in the butter and lard. Press into a dough, adding a little iced water if necessary to bind.

With two thirds of the pastry line small deep patty-pans. Chill. Preheat oven to 200°C/400°F/Gas 6. Trim off mushroom stalks, put the tops into a sieve and dip the mushrooms into boiling water. Drain them then pat dry and chop. Put them into a bowl and mix in the oil, cheese and seasonings. Fill the pastry cases with the mixture. Roll out the remaining pastry and make lids for the cases. Seal the lids with the beaten egg. Make a small x-cut in the centre of each lid. Bake in the oven for 15–18 minutes. Serve warm.

CDW

Guacamole

This famous Mexican avocado mash can be served as a first course with some brown toast, but is usually used as a dip – not a form of eating I particularly favour, but if you do, serve with corn chips or tortillas. Be warned: a hot chilli's fire is contained in its seeds and pale interior spines. To temper the chilli's pungency remove both with a sharp knife, but do not touch your face or eyes until you have washed your hands or you will be in agony.

2 good-sized avocados
2 tbsp finely chopped or grated Spanish onion
1 small hot green chilli, deseeded and finely chopped
4 sprigs of fresh coriander leaves, finely chopped
¼ tsp salt
1 large tomato, deseeded and chopped
2 tbsp finely chopped red onion
1 tbsp lime or lemon juice

Mix the Spanish onion, chilli, half the coriander and the salt in a mortar. Pound into a paste. Scoop the avocado flesh into a bowl. Mash the flesh well, then add the paste from the mortar. Mix thoroughly, and stir in the tomato, red onion and the rest of the coriander. Sprinkle the surface with the lime or lemon juice. Cover tightly with cling film and chill until wanted. Just before serving, give it a good stir and adjust seasoning.

JP

Corn Griddle Cakes

My mother was a great devotee of all things relating to the Southern States of America. After a dose of Francis Parkinson Keyes she would drive the cook mad with requests for recipes from 'Dixie', so with a cry of 'company's a comin' Miz Scarlett', the cook would retire to make these griddle cakes in the hopes that my father might object. He never did as he liked them, so we had them quite often. Finally, one of my sisters married a man from South Carolina, which cured my mother of her Dixie obsession. These should be cooked on a griddle, but if you do not have one, a heavy frying pan will do.

225g/8oz plain flour
1½ tsp baking powder
¼ tsp paprika
½ tsp salt
175g/6oz fresh sweetcorn kernels cut from the cob (frozen or tinned will do)
1 egg, beaten
125ml/4floz milk
2 tbsp melted butter

Sift the dry ingredients into a bowl. Combine the sweetcorn, egg and milk, add to the flour mixture and mix well. Then add the butter. Spoon on to a hot griddle, using 2 or 3 tbsp of the mixture for each cake. Cook until bubbles show on the surface, then turn the cakes over and cook the other sides until golden brown. They make a good breakfast dish served with crisp rashers of bacon and maple syrup, if liked.

CDW

Naxian Cheese Coins

This is a very good receipt I got from a cousin who lives in Naxos. They are the Naxian equivalent of cheese straws and are made with a local cheese called *kefalo tiri*. Maybe you could get it at a Greek delicatessen, but I do not have one so I use Parmesan instead. The main thing is that it should be a very hard cheese, so perhaps any old bits of Cheddar would do as long as it is grated very finely.

115g/4oz Parmesan, finely grated
115g/4oz butter, or margarine if preferred
115g/4oz plain flour
a large pinch of salt
½ tsp each paprika, celery salt and dry mustard
a large pinch of cayenne pepper
1 egg yolk

Keep the butter or margarine in the freezer at the ready. Sift the flour, salt and all the dry spices into a bowl. Add the cheese. Grate the frozen butter on the coarsest side of your grater and mix into the flour with a knife or fingertips until crumb-like. Beat the egg yolk and combine with the mixture to bind it. Knead everything together until pliable. Divide into three pieces. Roll each piece in the palms of your hands to form a sausage with the diameter of a large coin. Place the sausage shapes on a board and refrigerate for at least 2 hours.

Slice into thinnish discs. Arrange on oven trays and bake in a pre-heated oven at 190°C/375°F/Gas 5 for 10–15 minutes, swapping the tray positions at half time. The coins should be crisp and golden brown, and are perfectly splendid with a good cocktail.

JP

Cheese Soufflé Tartlets

These little creatures, taken from Margaret Costa's *Four Seasons Cookery Book*, should be served immediately, or at least still hot, or they lose their charm.

MAKES ABOUT 24

FOR THE PASTRY CASES:
225g/8oz self-raising flour
55g/2oz lard
55g/2oz butter

FOR THE SOUFFLÉ FILLING:
115g/4oz streaky bacon, finely chopped
1 medium onion, finely chopped
25g/1oz butter, melted
25g/1oz plain flour
150ml/¼ pint milk
salt and pepper
2 eggs, separated
115g/4oz cheese, grated

To make the pastry cases, sift the flour into a bowl and rub in the lard and butter. Press into a dough, adding a little iced water if necessary to bind. Use to line 5.5cm/2¼ in tartlet tins.

Fry the bacon gently in its own fat. Add the onion and fry gently until soft. Set aside.

To make a white sauce, melt the butter over a low heat, add the flour and cook over low heat for a minute or two, stirring all the time. Heat the milk, then gradually add it to the flour and butter roux, stirring constantly, over the low heat. Cook the sauce for about three minutes , then season well. Allow the mixture to cool slightly before beating in the egg yolks and grated cheese. Whisk the egg whites until stiff and fold into the cheese mixture. Divide the bacon and onion mixture among the pastry cases. Cover each with a spoonful of the soufflé mixture. Bake in a preheated oven at 200°C/400°F/Gas 6 for 20 minutes.

JP

Illustrated overleaf

FISH AND SHELLFISH

Buying monkfish on the quay at Mevagissey, in Cornwall

I am tempted to say unless you have a good fishmonger don't bother. As Jennifer says, if it smells of fish it isn't fresh. Surrounded as we are by water, we are terribly served for fish. My sister once lived in the centre of Spain, and the fish lorries came up from the coast three times a week with live fish. Here, the average fishmonger in large towns, when you can find one, offers a limited choice, and the fish is not always in its first flush of freshness. Supermarket fish is usually a disgrace and a victim of some central buying and distribution policy, which means it has travelled the country more times than Jennifer and I have in our TV series! The most useful tool in judging the freshness of fish is the nose, quickly

followed by the eyes. The chances of your being allowed to smell an individual fish in a supermarket are slight, but you can challenge your fishmonger who will usually permit you. Of course, if you make a friend of him you won't need to check.

Neither of us much believe the pronouncements of *soi-disant* health experts – we both eat fish because we love it, the fresher the better. So for once we are not out of step with these 'experts' in believing in the health benefits of fish. We have seen some wonderful fish during our travels, such as the underrated coley which Jennifer turned into a luscious fish pie. Coley is still amazingly underpriced and very good.

Jennifer lets Clarissa carry a coley

never understand people who want everything cooked before people arrive – some of my most pleasant dalliances have been conducted in my kitchen during a dinner party! And anyway I'm not that keen on casseroles. In this age of fisharians (i.e. vegetarians who eat fish) the ability to cook it well is of great importance. We are always being told how good oily fish is for us and eating it is so much nicer than swallowing a spoonful of cod liver oil. It is also important to try the different range of fish available. So many people just stick to cod, haddock or salmon, but don't be afraid to experiment and ask your fishmonger what is particularly good or in season – remember fish have seasons, just like fruit and vegetables, so buy accordingly.

We've also seen the hideous monkfish, the true denizen of the deep with its huge head and delicious flesh, ling, cod, John Dory – still bearing St Peter's thumb print – the sad-faced little gurnards which Jennifer loves so much, and so many more, the list is endless.

There are really only two things to remember with fish: buy it as fresh as possible and please don't overcook it – it is better to err on the side of caution and undercook it because a very hot serving dish can easily remedy that situation. I like to serve a separate fish course at a dinner party but most people will have it as a main course. It is a good choice if you are eating late as it is easily digestible and takes no time to cook. The trick with fish is to make your guests wait for it rather than the other way round. I

Cooking mussels in the pouring rain on Hemmick Beach

Fish Stew

You can use any fish in this receipt but I flavour the fleshier ones such as monk, coley and red mullet which all give a good flavour. Ask your fishmonger to fillet and clean them. If you like you can add spoonfuls of aioli to the finished stew, once in the bowl.

750g/1½lb assorted fish, cut into chunks
1 tbsp olive oil
25g/1oz butter
1 large onion, chopped
1 large leek, white part only, chopped
2 celery sticks, de-fibred and chopped
2 cloves of garlic, finely chopped
115g/¼lb mushrooms, finely sliced
2 potatoes, peeled and chopped
3 large tomatoes, skinned and chopped
150ml/5fl oz white wine
300ml/10fl oz water
1 bouquet garni
2 bayleaves
salt and freshly ground pepper
1 tbsp chopped parsley
pinch of saffron

Fry onion, leek, celery, garlic, mushrooms and potatoes in the oil and butter until the onion begins to brown. Add the chopped tomatoes. Add the fish. Cover with wine and water. Add the bouquet garni, bayleaves and salt and pepper to taste. Bring to the boil and simmer for 12–15 minutes. Add the parsley and the saffron before serving.

JP

Halibut in Cider

This is a good summer dish. Halibut is a very under-used fish. Don't let your fishmonger cut the cutlets too thin, and be sure to use dry cider.

4 halibut cutlets
225g/8oz onions, chopped
2 tbsp olive oil
1 clove of garlic, crushed
600ml/1 pint dry cider
salt and freshly ground pepper
2 lemons
450g/1lb ripe tomatoes, peeled and sliced
a handful of finely chopped parsley
butter

Sauté the onions gently in the oil till pale gold. Add the garlic and cook a little longer. Stir in the cider, and add salt and pepper to taste.

Put the halibut cutlets in a greased ovenproof dish, season and add the juice of 1 lemon. Thinly slice the remaining lemon and arrange over the fish. Pour the onions and cider over the fish. Place the tomatoes and chopped parsley on top and dot with butter.

Bake in a preheated oven at 180°C/350°F/Gas 4 for 20 minutes. Serve hot.

CDW

Fresh Grilled Tuna Salad

During a shoot we tend to eat rather a lot and rather late. There is nothing I like more on my return to my flat in Victoria than a simple salad Niçoise. I always feel that there is something very restorative about it.

1 tuna steak per person, about 2.5cm/1 inch thick
olive oil
350g/12oz baby new potatoes
115g/4oz green beans
10 lettuce leaves – Cos or similar
3 hard-boiled eggs, quartered
225g/8oz cherry tomatoes
8 anchovy fillets
12 black olives
1 red onion, thickly sliced
55g/2oz salted butter
3 garlic cloves
1 tbsp balsamic vinegar
4–5 tbsp olive oil
2 tbsp chopped chervil
salt and pepper

You can grill the tuna but it is far better cooked on a griddle; turn both ways to achieve that criss-cross pattern. Grill or griddle the tuna for about 1½ minutes in total, so that it is still pink in the middle. If you prefer it well done, cook for 1½ minutes each side. Par-boil the baby potatoes and then sauté in a pan with the butter and one clove of garlic until golden. Pour the oil into a jug and add the rest of the garlic, chervil, and salt and pepper. Slowly whisk in the balsamic vinegar and stand the mixture aside. Boil the beans for 3½ minutes. Drain and run under cold water. Chop the beans in half. Place the tomatoes, the potatoes and the beans and the red onion into a salad bowl and drizzle half the vinaigrette onto this. Toss thoroughly and serve with the tuna steak on top of the salad.

JP

Turbot with Watercress and Pickled Walnuts

I make people down south tired with my endless praise for the wonderful fish in my beloved Scotland, and more especially for my joy in the friendship of my dear Mr Clark who dispenses such delights in Fisherrow, Musselburgh. Turbot is a great fish. People complain that it is too expensive, but it is so firm and meaty that you don't need as much of it as less satisfying fish. You can do this dish with a 900g/2lb chicken turbot, but it is more usual to make it with one 175g/6oz steak per person.

4 turbot steaks (175g/6oz each)
115g/4oz sliced onions
about 450ml/¾ pint mixed white wine and fish stock
12 pickled walnuts, plus extra to garnish
55g/2oz butter
a bunch of watercress, finely chopped
salt and freshly ground pepper

Put the turbot steaks in a pan with the onions and enough wine and stock to cover. Bring to the boil, then poach gently for 15 minutes. Remove the fish to a serving dish and keep warm. Strain the liquid and reserve.

Mash the pickled walnuts. Combine them with the butter, 300ml/½ pint of the fish cooking liquid and the chopped watercress. Season. Bring to the boil and simmer for a few minutes. Pour this sauce over the fish, garnish with pickled walnut halves and serve.

CDW

Turbot Kebabs with Tomato and Cumin Sauce

Turbot is very expensive and a great treat, one of the noblest of fish. Alternatively, you could use another firm fish for these kebabs, such as halibut, monkfish or even the humble coley.

675–900g/1½–2 lb skinned and filleted turbot
2 tbsp olive oil
juice of half a lemon
salt and freshly ground pepper
bayleaves

FOR THE SAUCE:
1 large onion, chopped
1 clove of garlic, chopped
25g/1oz unsalted butter
1 tbsp olive oil
a 400g/14oz tin plum tomatoes, drained
1 tsp chilli powder
1 tsp ground cumin
1 tbsp honey
salt and freshly ground pepper
150ml/¼ pint double cream

Cut the turbot into 2.5–4cm/1–1½in cubes. Mix together the olive oil, lemon juice, salt and pepper and pour over the fish. Cover and leave to marinate for half an hour.

To make the sauce, fry the chopped onion and garlic in the butter and olive oil gently until the onion is translucent. Add the drained tomatoes, chilli powder and cumin. Stir, then leave to simmer for 45 minutes, stirring occasionally. Purée in a blender or food processor. Add the honey and season with salt and pepper. Allow to cool. Add the cream and warm through for serving, but do not allow to boil.

Thread the cubes of fish and bayleaves alternately on to skewers. Cook under a preheated hot grill, turning occasionally. Serve with the tomato and cumin sauce.

JP

Fish Pie

Like most people, I always welcome fish pie as one of the most comforting of foods. This is rather a grandiose one and is splendid to eat on Good Friday after a day of fasting, or on Christmas Eve before midnight mass, or for that matter any time you fancy it.

450 g/1lb coley fillet
450 g/1lb smoked haddock fillet
6 scallops
225g/8oz fresh peeled cooked prawns
1–1.3kg/2–3lb fresh spinach
115g/4oz butter plus extra for the top
salt and freshly ground pepper
grated nutmeg
1 large Spanish onion, thinly sliced
3 tbsp plain flour
1½ pints milk
1 bayleaf
4 tsp anchovy essence
a big bunch of parsley, chopped
115g/4oz Parmesan, freshly grated

Put the coley and smoked haddock into a large pan and pour boiling water over just to cover. Simmer very gently for 10 minutes. Turn it all out into a clean sink and leave until the fish is cool enough to handle. Then remove skin and any bones. Flake the fish on to a plate and reserve.

Wash the spinach thoroughly and place in a saucepan – do not add any water. Cook gently until it collapses, then raise the heat and cook until done, about 3 minutes. Drain well, pressing the liquid out. Return the spinach to the saucepan with 55g/2oz butter and season to taste with salt, pepper and nutmeg. Spread the spinach evenly on the bottom of a well-buttered oven dish large enough to take the rest of the ingredients.

Melt the remaining 55g/2oz of butter in a saucepan and cook the onion gently until translucent. Add the flour and stir round to make a roux. Have the milk heated to a simmer and add it little by little until you have a smooth béchamel sauce. Pop in the bayleaf and let it simmer for half an hour, stirring now and then.

Stir the anchovy essence and parsley into the sauce, and season with salt and pepper. Mix in the flaked fish and pour on to the spinach. Slice the whites of the scallops in half horizontally and distribute over the fish, interspersed with their corals. Scatter the prawns over the top, sprinkle with the Parmesan and dot with a little extra butter. Bake in a preheated oven at 200°C/400°F/Gas 6 for 20–30 minutes until heated through and browned on the top. Serve with a purée of potato and a tomato salad.

JP

Kedgeree

Hindi 'khichri', the original kedgeree, is a dish of boiled rice and lentils. I imagine a little Bombay duck was added at some point to give the fishy part, and when the dish was brought home to England by some old colonel at the beginning of the nineteenth century, smoked haddock was substituted. Kedgeree became the mainstay of Victorian breakfasts, with the lentils eschewed entirely and eggs added. It is the most comforting dish in the world.

450g/1lb smoked haddock
1 medium onion, finely chopped
115g/4oz butter
1 tsp garam masala
½ tsp turmeric
350g/12oz basmati rice
4 hard-boiled eggs, 2 roughly chopped and 2 quartered
300ml/½ pint single cream, warmed (optional)
salt and freshly ground pepper
1 tbsp chopped parsley

Simmer the haddock in salted water for 10–15 minutes, but don't over cook. Drain the fish, saving the cooking water. Remove the skin and bones, and flake the fish; keep hot. Fry the onion gently in the butter with the garam masala and turmeric until softened. Cook the rice in the haddock water until tender, then drain and allow to dry out a little. Add the spiced fried onion to the rice, and fold in the flaked fish and the roughly chopped eggs. Pour in the cream and add the quartered eggs. Season with salt and pepper, and sprinkle the parsley over all.

JP

Hake Portuguese

Both the Portuguese and the Spanish have a passion for hake. It is a very good fish though not used much by the British – pray go out and buy some. It is also very good cold, covered in mayonnaise and served with a beautiful potato salad.

4 x 225g/½lb cuts of hake
115g/4oz butter
2 tbsp olive oil
8 shallots, finely chopped
450g/1lb tomatoes, skinned, de-seeded and chopped
1 yellow pepper, skinned, de-seeded and chopped
1 tbsp frozen peas
115g/4oz cooked (al dente) rice
2 tbsp chopped parsley
2 glasses white wine
salt and freshly ground pepper

Heat 25g/1oz butter with the olive oil in an ovenproof dish, add the shallots and fry until the shallots are translucent. Lay the fish on top of the cooked shallots and dot with knobs of the remaining butter. Cover the fish with chopped tomatoes, yellow pepper, frozen peas and surround the fish with the rice and chopped parsley. Pour in the wine, add salt and pepper and bake in a moderate oven at 190°C/375°F/Gas 5/ for 30–35 minutes.

JP

Ham 'n' Haddie

One of Scotland's greatest contributions to the enjoyment of food is cold smoked fish, and the pale opalescent hue of an undyed smoked haddock on the breakfast table is a great joy. Even Dr Johnson, who was not noted for his love of Scotland, rightly remarked, 'If a man would breakfast well he must breakfast in Scotland'. Finnan haddies take their name from Findon in Kincardineshire, where the fish wives hung their dried salted haddocks in their chimneys to smoke over their peat fires. A Finnan haddie is a whole cured fish, bones and all, and is the smoked haddock to use for this dish. It is a traditional Scot's breakfast dish, which can equally well be eaten for high tea.

SERVES 6

25g/1oz butter
2 large slices of ham, cut from the bone
2 large smoked haddock
150ml/¼ pint milk
freshly ground black pepper
150ml/¼ pint double cream

Heat the butter in a large pan and lightly fry the ham, turning once; remove and cut into 6 pieces. Place the haddock in the pan and cover with the milk. Bring to the boil and simmer for 2 minutes on each side. Lift out the fish, remove skin and bones, and divide the flesh into 6 pieces. Strain the milk and reserve. Return the ham to the pan, place the haddock pieces on top and gently pour over the milk. Season with pepper. Cover and simmer gently for 3 minutes. Pour the cream evenly over the surface, and brown under a pre-heated hot grill.

CDW

Smoked Haddock and Lovage Tart

This recipe comes from *Feasting on Herbs,* an excellent book by my dear friend Sue Lawrence who is one of the best cooks I know. I cooked it untested for a dinner of Gaelic poets and it was much praised by the late great Sorley Maclean. As he was speaking Gaelic at the time I can't tell you what he said. It is excellent, and I know you will love it.

FOR THE PASTRY:
150g/6oz plain flour
55g/2oz polenta
salt
115g/4oz unsalted butter
1 egg combined
1 tbsp olive oil

FOR THE FILLING:
350g/12 oz undyed smoked haddock
150ml/¼ pint milk
150ml/¼ pint cream
3 eggs
2 tbsp lovage
salt and freshly ground pepper

To make your pastry in a food processor, mix all the dried ingredients, chop in the butter then add the egg and oil, spinning until a paste forms. Chill for 30 minutes. Roll out and line a 23cm/9in flan tin. The pastry will be very crumbly so patch it in by hand and chill in the tin for a further 30 minutes. Bake blind in a preheated oven 190°C/375°F/Gas 5 until the pastry is cooked and pale gold, 15–20 minutes. Cool slightly.

Poach the fish in the milk, remove from milk and flake into pie crust reserving the milk. Whisk the cream and eggs into the milk and add the lovage, season and pour over the fish. Return to the oven and bake for 30 minutes or until the filling is set. Cool slightly before serving. This is also good cold.

CDW

Trout Quenelles with Watercress Sauce

Although as my friend Angus quite rightly, if somewhat acerbically, pointed out the French only make *quenelles* with pike, trout is an excellent substitute. It is also one which I served at a ten-course dinner party I once cooked in an alcoholic blackout so you can see that it is not difficult.

275g/10oz fresh trout
275g/10oz smoked trout
3 egg whites
a pinch of mace
salt and pepper
300ml/½ pint double cream

FOR THE SAUCE:
5 tbsp finely chopped shallot
150ml/¼ pint dry white wine
150ml/¼ pint strong chicken stock
300ml/½ pint whipping cream
4 bunches watercress
lemon juice to taste
55g/2oz butter

Put into a food processor all the fish and blend until smooth, add the egg whites and blend until completely smooth. Add salt and pepper and mace, pour in the cream with the machine running, do not run the machine for more than 20 seconds. Don't let the mixture get too thin, it must sit up on a spoon. Chill for 30 minutes.

Bring a wide pan of salted water to a simmer. Dip a dessertspoon in warm water and take a good rounded spoonful of the mixture. Use another spoon to form the quenelle. Poach each quenelle in the water for 8–10 minutes, remove with a slotted spoon and drain on kitchen paper. Put in a warm dish and when all are made pour over sauce and serve at once.

To make the sauce, simmer the shallot and the wine together for 15 minutes or more until it forms a soft purée and the wine is almost evaporated. Add stock and cream, season and boil until reduced by one third and coating a spoon. Pick over the watercress discarding tough stalks and discoloured leaves and toss into a pan of boiling salted water. Blanch for 2–3 minutes, drain and refresh under a cold tap. Squeeze out excess water. In the food processor purée the watercress for 1–2 minutes until a smooth purée is formed, pour the hot cream over the purée and process adding the lemon juice and the butter in small pieces. Strain and reheat without boiling, pour over quenelles and serve at once.

CDW

Trout in Rosé de Loire

A lovely pink trout with a lovely pink sauce. A very suitable dish for mid Lent or a mid Advent Sunday when priests always wear pink vestments.

4 medium-sized trout, boned and gutted
115g/4oz butter
4 shallots, chopped
600ml/1 pint Rosé de Loire
1 bouquet garni
salt and freshly ground pepper
4 egg yolks
300ml/½ pint double cream
1 tbsp pink lumpfish
1 tbsp croûtons

Ask the fishmonger to gut and bone the trout. Melt half the butter in a frying pan and gently sauté the chopped shallots, do not burn. Add the trout and cook gently until lightly brown on both sides. Butter an ovenproof dish with half the remaining butter. Place the trout in the dish, add the wine, bouquet garni, salt and pepper. Dot each fish with knobs of the remaining butter and cook in a medium preheated oven 180°C/350°F/Gas 4 for 25–30 minutes, basting once or twice. Place fish on a serving plate and keep warm.

Pour the residual juices into a small saucepan and boil rapidly until reduced by half. Allow to cool for 2 minutes. Whisk the egg yolks with the cream and slowly add the juices while continuing to whisk. When the mixture is light and frothy, pour over the fish and serve immediately, garnished with lumpfish roe and croûtons.

JP

Cumberland Shipped Herring

My father grew up in Glasgow where Loch Fyne herrings, which were the fattest and best, were known as Glasgow Magistrates. Thanks to my friend, Johnny Noble, Loch Fyne herrings are once again flourishing. If you are driving up the west coast of Scotland don't miss a stop at Johnny's seafood restaurant at Cairndow; it is worth a detour.

As a child, I used to go to the West of Scotland for holidays, and herrings were staple fare. This dish is from Cumberland, further down the west coast, a strange remote area that until 1294 was part of Scotland and which remained very remote until Victorian times. Herrings are now hard to come by unless asked for in your fishmonger (not supermarket). Remember, they are very good for you.

4 fresh herrings
4 herring roes
15g/½oz breadcrumbs
2 tsp anchovy essence
1 small onion, chopped
1 tbsp melted butter
salt and freshly ground pepper
55g/2oz butter

Clean the herrings, and remove heads, tails, fins and backbones (a fishmonger will do this for you). Gently poach the herring roes in hot water for a few minutes. Drain and chop, then mix with the breadcrumbs, anchovy essence, onion, melted butter and seasoning to taste. Stuff the herrings with the mixture and secure each with a wooden cocktail stick. Lay the fish side by side in a buttered baking dish and dot with the butter. Bake in a preheated oven at 180°C/350°F/Gas 4 for about 20 minutes.

CDW

Cod Fillet in Mushroom, Shrimp and Cheese Sauce

Far from being the cheapest fish as it was not so many years ago, cod has now reached its rightful place in the menus of every grand restaurant.

4 thick cod fillets
115g/4oz butter
55g/2oz plain flour
300ml/½ pint milk
300ml/½ pint fish stock
115g/4oz mushrooms, halved
85g/3oz strong Cheddar cheese, grated
1 tsp anchovy essence
1 tbsp chopped parsley
salt and freshly ground pepper
225g/8oz cooked shrimps

Melt half the butter in a saucepan, add the flour, stir, and allow to bubble for 2 or 3 minutes, but be careful not to let it burn. Remove from heat. Butter a baking dish with 12g/½oz butter and place the cod fillets in it, cover with the fish stock and cook in a preheated moderate oven 190°C/370°F/Gas 5 for 15 minutes. Strain off the fish stock, add to the milk and gradually add this to the saucepan containing the flour and butter. Bring slowly to the boil, stirring gently, to get a smooth consistency.

Sauté the mushrooms in the remaining butter, add to your sauce with 25g/1oz of the cheese and the anchovy essence. Stir until cheese has melted, season to taste. Cut the fish into bite-size pieces. Add the shrimps and parsley to the fish in the baking dish, pour the sauce over the fish shaking the dish gently for the sauce to sink. Place the dish in a preheated oven at 200°C/400°F/Gas 6 for 10 minutes. Sprinkle over the remaining cheese, and put under a hot grill for a few minutes for the cheese to melt and brown.

JP

Gigot of Monkfish Romarin with Anchovies

I love monkfish tail and I love it with anchovies. The edge with rosemary comes from Pat Llewellyn in her cook's hat. The Scots, who have adopted the word gigot with gusto and even talk of 'gigit chops' for leg cuts of meat, have long attached this term to monkfish. The haute cuisine chefs were further behind.

a 1kg/2¼lb monkfish tail
1 tin anchovy fillets
6 tbsp olive oil
juice of 1 lemon
salt and freshly ground pepper
a large bunch of fresh rosemary

FOR THE TOMATO VINAIGRETTE:
10 tbsp olive oil
4 tsp wine vinegar
2 dessertspoons finely chopped tomatoes

Using a larding needle or a sharp knife, make slits in the fish and insert pieces of anchovy. Marinate the fish in a mixture of oil and lemon juice, seasoned with salt and pepper, for at least 2 hours.

Lay the fish on a large bed of rosemary in a roasting tin. Pour more oil over the fish. (It is the presence of fat that releases the essential oils of the rosemary.) Roast the fish in a preheated oven at 180°C/350°F/Gas 4 for 45 minutes.

To make the tomato vinaigrette, heat the ingredients in a small pan and season to taste. Transfer the fish to a serving dish and pour over the warm vinaigrette.

CDW

Illustrated overleaf

Marrow Stuffed with Salmon

This dish was inspired by a letter from my Hungarian barrister friend John Zeigler who wrote to admonish me on my misrepresentation of Rigo Jancsi chocolate slices. In the letter he referred to a Hungarian way of serving marrow with salmon. This isn't it but it is a fun dish all the same.

225g/8oz salmon
salt and freshly ground pepper
55g/2oz cooked rice
1 tbsp chopped pickled cucumber
1 tbsp sour cream
1 tbsp chopped dill
1 medium-sized marrow
25g/1oz butter

In a frying pan briefly sauté the salmon until you can flake it. Season well. Mix the salmon with the other ingredients. Cut a cap from the broad end of the marrow and hollow out, removing the seeds and some flesh. Rub the inside of the marrow with pepper. Fill with the filling. Replace the cap and secure with some tin foil. Place in a baking dish, brush with butter, cover with foil and bake in a preheated oven at 180°C/350°F/Gas 4 for 1–1½ hours.

CDW

Roasted Salmon with Scallops and Mustard Butter

I can't tell you how good this is. I was introduced to it by Guy Harrington, one of our dear researchers, who in his day ran many a restaurant or strummed the piano in far off bars. We had it as a starter, but it could be a splendid main course with a few new potatoes.

900g/2lb salmon middle cut, boned, or fillets
150g/6oz butter
8 scallops, without roe
3 generous tsp wholegrain mustard
4 level tsp dried dill weed, or 2 tsp each of dried and fresh dill
salt and freshly ground pepper
275g/10oz fresh spinach or rocket

Preheat the oven to 230°C/450°F/Gas 8. Place the salmon piece or fillets skin-side up in a shallow ovenproof dish. Cook in the oven for 15 minutes. Meanwhile gently melt the butter in a small saucepan. Remove from the heat and stir in the mustard and dill. Season to taste. Remove the salmon from the oven and place the scallops round it, baste with the mustard sauce. Return to the oven for a further 5 minutes. Slice the salmon quite thickly and serve on top of the spinach or rocket and spoon over the mustard butter.

JP

Illustrated overleaf

Lady Llanover's Salmon

Our beloved Pat Llewellyn is convinced that only the Welsh cook salmon in red wine. She may be right. Certainly the renowned Lady Llanover did. It adds a richness to the fish that is quite unique.

a 900g/2lb piece of middle-cut salmon, skinned
85g/3oz butter
25g/1oz plain flour
1 onion, chopped
450g/1lb mushrooms, sliced
1 clove of garlic, crushed
a sprig of fresh rosemary
½ bottle of red wine

Work 25g/1oz of the butter with the flour into a paste (*beurre manié*) and set aside. Fry the onion and mushrooms in the remaining butter. When soft, add the garlic and rosemary. Pour the fried onion mixture into a casserole, add the skinned salmon, pour the red wine over and leave to marinate for 2 hours.

Put the casserole on the hob or gas ring, bring the liquid to the boil and simmer gently for 15 minutes. Lift out the salmon and fillet it, but leave it in one piece. Keep warm. Strain the sauce and return it to the casserole. Reduce the sauce, gradually adding the *beurre manié* until it is the consistency of thin cream.

Put the strained vegetables from the casserole in a serving dish, place the salmon on top and pour over the sauce. Serve hot.

CDW

A Lobster for Lady Strathmore

As the result of a rather jolly meeting in a bread shop, Jennifer and I went to Glamis to demonstrate. Isobel, the present Countess, had decided that pineapples were a better bet than flowers in mid-winter Scotland and the whole house was decorated with them. Glamis is a splendid castle, and she and her husband were splendid hosts, so I thought I would invent a splendid dish in remembrance of the occasion.

2 live lobsters (about 675g/
1½ lb each)
1 large pineapple
55g/2oz unsalted butter
2 shallots, finely chopped
300ml/½ pint double cream
salt and freshly ground pepper
55g/2oz capers
2 sun-dried tomatoes

Cook the lobsters using your approved method. I put mine into lukewarm water, bring to the boil and cook for 10 minutes to each 450g/1lb. Remove the lobster meat from the shells and cut into 2.5cm/1in chunks.

Cut the pineapple in half from top to bottom and scoop out the flesh, hollowing out the shell halves but leaving them intact. Squeeze the juice from the flesh, then discard the flesh. Melt half of the butter in a saucepan and gently fry the shallots until they just colour. Add the cream, bring to the boil and reduce by one third. Add the lobster meat and half the pineapple juice, season and bring back to the boil. Stir in the capers and tomatoes. Divide the mixture between the two pineapple halves. Dot with the remaining butter, and put under a preheated hot grill for 5 minutes or until the surface is golden.

CDW

Lobster with Latkas

I have an unlimited passion for lobsters which I do very well with, thanks to my dear Mr Clark of Fisherrow, Musselburgh, the best fishmonger in Britain. I also love latkas, those crispy mouth watering Jewish potato pancakes. So it seemed to me an excellent idea to combine the two.

4 boiled lobsters
85g/3oz butter
115g/4oz shallots, sliced
140g/5oz mushrooms, sliced
150ml/¼ pint whisky
freshly ground black pepper
pinch of ground cloves
300ml/½ pint double cream

FOR THE LATKAS:
900g/2lb potatoes, peeled and finely grated
225g/8oz onion, grated
150g/6oz matzo meal, use flour if not available
4 eggs
2 tsp caraway seeds
salt and freshly ground pepper
oil for frying

Remove the meat from the lobsters and cut into pieces. Melt 55g/2oz butter and fry the shallots until soft, add the mushrooms and cook gently, then add the lobster and mix well. Cover and cook very gently for 3 minutes. Warm the whisky, set it alight and, when the flames have died down, pour over the lobster. Season with black pepper and cloves and add the cream. Shake over the heat until well-mixed, cover and cook over a very gentle flame for 5 minutes.

To make the latkas, wash the grated potatoes in several changes of cold water to remove excess starch. Pat dry with a towel and mix with the rest of the ingredients. Season well. Heat the oil in a large frying pan, drop tablespoons of the mixture into the hot oil. Flatten each dollop into a round small flat pancake. Fry on medium heat for 3–4 minutes on each side until the pancake is a pale golden brown and perfectly crisp. Drain on absorbent paper and serve very hot with the lobster. If you are being stylish you can stack the latkas with lobster sandwiched between and the sauce drizzled round the base of the stack.

CDW

Cerveach of Sole

Not to be confused with the South American ceviche, this old way of dressing fish requires the fish to be cooked first. I demonstrated it at a Georgian cooking forum, and thereafter found I was being served it all over Edinburgh. Do try it.

4 fillets of sole
oil
salt and freshly ground pepper
1 onion, sliced into thin rings
fresh herbs

FOR THE DRESSING:
125ml/4floz olive oil
2 tbsp white wine vinegar
shredded rind and juice of 1 lemon
2 bayleaves

Heat a film of cooking oil in a frying pan. Flatten each fish fillet with a rolling pin. Sprinkle on some salt and pepper and fold in half. Fry gently and briefly on both sides.

Arrange the fish on a long dish and scatter the onion rings over the top. Mix the dressing ingredients together and pour over the fish whilst it is still hot. Leave for at least 3 hours to cool. Serve at room temperature, garnished with herbs.

CDW

Sole in Vermouth

Vermouth is always good with fish, having a stronger flavour than any white wine and, as I'm not tempted to drink it on its own, I always seem to have some. Sole is one of the finest fish but alas now very expensive. However, we all deserve a great treat every now and then. So enjoy.

8 fillets of sole
3 shallots, finely chopped
150g/6oz butter
2 tbsp parsley, finely chopped
1 tbsp fresh tarragon
dry vermouth
juice of ½ a lemon
salt and freshly ground pepper

Soften shallots in 55g/2oz of butter in a large ovenproof dish and add parsley and tarragon. Place fish fillets on top of shallots and herbs and season with salt and pepper. Pour in sufficient vermouth to come level with the fish. Dot fish with 55g/2oz butter. Cook in preheated hot oven at 220°C/425°F/Gas 7 for 20–30 minutes or until the fish flakes easily.

Remove the fish to hot serving dish, pour juices into a saucepan and reduce rapidly to half. Remove the pan from the heat and whisk in remaining butter, taste for seasoning, add a squeeze of lemon juice and pour the sauce over fish.

JP

Singapore Prawns with Bugis Street Sauce

I haven't been back to Singapore since 1948 but I always remember those marvellous prawn dishes I had in Bugis Street. This recipe is the nearest I can get to one of the sauces. There was always a side dish of small red chillies and one of our friends would chew these as if he was eating peanuts. The more reserved of us would take one or two.

750g/1½lb cooked and shelled prawns
2 tbsp vegetable oil
115g/4oz mushrooms, sliced
4 tbsp chopped spring onions
1 clove of garlic, chopped
1 tsp grated fresh ginger
1½ tbsp hoison sauce
1½ tbsp oyster sauce
2 tsp red Thai curry paste
pinch of five spice powder
300ml/10fl oz coconut milk
salt and pepper

Heat the vegetable oil in wok or frying pan, put in the mushrooms, spring onions, garlic and ginger for a couple of minutes. Add the hoisin sauce, oyster sauce, red curry paste and five spice powder and stir well. Then add the coconut milk, a little salt and pepper and the prawns. Simmer gently for 1–2 minutes and serve on a bed of rice or noodles.

JP

MEAT

Happy Gloucester Old Spots out in the mud

I am happy to report that in the last couple of years a number of vegetarians have been restored to the fold of meat eaters. I have never been able to understand the reasoning that if you don't like the way meat is reared or killed you turn vegetarian. Surely you should stand up and fight for changes and support the organic trade rather than risk your life with a paraquat-fed Third World carrot. Anyone who saw the quality of the Prince of Wales cattle herd when we filmed at Highgrove, and observed how happy and confident they were, would agree with me.

Jennifer has made the point that you can't really digest pork without its fat, but people forget this when buying meat. I will never forget a pig farmer who told me that the supermarkets are demanding leaner and leaner beasts and as a result the pigs have no natural protection against extremes of weather and get sunburnt very easily. We once filmed with a lot of very happy Gloucester Old Spot pigs in the Cotswolds and it was great to see the boar and the sow lying about soaking up the sun. The farmer said that the young pigs needed a mud wallow from time to time to escape the danger of sunburn, which makes me worry for those so-called happy pigs standing around in shadeless fields.

What a wealth of variety we have lost with the unification of breeds of sheep. When I prepared a lunch for the Duke of Hamilton and his

Trustees at Lennoxlove House, I complained to my butcher that the chops he was offering were too large for what I required. 'Well,' he replied, 'we'll just have to take them from a black-face sheep, they'll be smaller!' Mutton is a strong flavour and we live increasingly in a country where the only acceptable strong flavour is a vindaloo curry. Curiously the only people in Britain who really still eat mutton are the Asian community. I was interested to see on the menu in a balti house both curried lamb and curried mutton; elsewhere we have lost such distinctions of palate. What a bland and tasteless world we are heading towards so terrifyingly fast. Our views on beef are well known, and I don't want to bore you with reiteration, so I

When it comes to meat, Jennifer and Clarissa are deadly serious

Outside the shop of butcher Jesse Smith in Cirencester, 'A carnivore's delight'

shall merely make the point that British beef is now the safest in the world. What a shame that when we went to Smithfield this year we couldn't buy the same cut on the bone.

Both Jennifer and I agree that with meat of any kind the trick is to buy the best you can afford. Don't waste good money on cheap fillet steak, which may be poorly hung, when for the same or less money you can get a beautiful piece of rump which will taste much better. Again, make friends with your butcher – he will tell you what is good. I am always amazed to discover how little one pays for the cheaper cuts and how much better some of them taste than expensive meat. The proof is in the eating.

Roast Meat Loaf or 'Hedgehog'

I evolved this robust, strongly flavoured monster when I had to feed a lot of people at a curious school in Padworth. It is excellent for picnics, parties and christenings, let alone wakes.

450g/1lb each minced beef, minced pork and minced veal or turkey
225g/8oz chicken or turkey livers
450g/1lb best sausage meat
225g/8oz good mushrooms, sliced
butter
salt and freshly ground pepper
grated nutmeg
1 large onion, grated
3 fat cloves of garlic, crushed to a paste
10 juniper berries, crushed
1 good tsp ground allspice
sprigs of fresh thyme
1–2 eggs
225g/8oz rashers of unsmoked streaky bacon
bayleaves
branches of fresh rosemary

Sauté the mushrooms in butter until the juices run, then season with salt and pepper plus a good grating of nutmeg. Reserve. Remove the sinews from the livers and slice. In a large bowl combine all the minced meats, the sausage meat, the livers, the onion, garlic and juniper berries. Add the allspice and some thyme leaves. Season with salt and about 20 turns of the pepper mill. Beat the egg(s) and add to the mixture together with the mushrooms. Use your spotless hands to mix this whole lot together most thoroughly.

Oil a roasting tin and place all the mixture in it, moulding it into an oval shape. Adorn with the rashers of bacon, criss-crossed Union Jack style, tucking the ends under the meat loaf. Strew some bayleaves and branches of rosemary on the top and sides. Cook in a preheated oven at 230°C/450°F/Gas 8 for 15 minutes, then lower the heat to 180°C/350°F/Gas 4 and cook for a further 1½ hours.

When cooked, there will be lots of lovely juices in the bottom of the tin; save them for flavouring soup, stock or an egg dish. Remove the loaf and place on a good dish. Serve hot or cold with a good tomato sauce made from fresh or tinned tomatoes in the Italian manner.

For children, you might like to turn it into a 'hedgehog' by pressing almonds into the meat to create prickles and placing 3 olives at one end to form eyes and a nose. This should be done before putting into the oven.

JP

Collared Beef

This is a very good dish served cold, for a buffet. It can also be served hot with a dill or horseradish sauce. Collared beef is so called because it is served in the shape of a collar.

a 1–1.8kg/2–4lb salt flank or
boned rib of beef
2 tbsp chopped parsley
½ tsp each chopped fresh sage,
dried mixed herbs, cayenne
pepper and grated nutmeg or
ground allspice
salt and freshly ground pepper

Remove any gristle from the meat. Mix together all the herbs and spices. Coat the inside of the meat with the mixture, roll up tightly and tie with string. Wrap in a cloth, preferably muslin.

Set the joint in a saucepan, cover with cold water and bring to the boil. Reduce the heat and simmer for half an hour to each 450g/1lb.

Remove the beef from the pan. Put a heavy weight on the meat, without removing the cloth, and press until cold. The best way to do this is to put a board over the meat and load it with weights or cans of food. To serve, unwrap the meat and slice it thinly.

CDW

Brisket of Beef with Onion Sauce

Get your brisket from a good butcher. It should be interlined with fat, not a nasty little knob of meat as is found in supermarkets.

a 1.35kg/3lb brisket of beef
salt
1 large onion, cut into quarters
a couple of parsley and thyme sprigs
2 carrots, cut into chunks
2 bayleaves
1 small turnip, cut up
12 peppercorns

FOR THE ONION SAUCE:
450g/1lb onions, chopped
85g/3oz butter
40g/1½ oz plain flour
450ml/¾ pint stock (from the brisket cooking water)
150ml/¼ pint milk
ground mace
freshly grated nutmeg
salt and freshly ground pepper

Place the brisket in a large saucepan with all the other ingredients and cover with water. Bring to the boil, then lower the heat and simmer gently for 2½–3 hours.

Towards the end of the brisket cooking time, make the sauce. Cook the onions gently in 55g/2oz of the butter until they are translucent; set aside to cool. Make a roux of the remaining butter and the flour, and gradually add the stock (taken from the water in which the brisket is cooking) and milk, stirring all the time. Bring to the boil. Add a pinch each of mace and nutmeg. Turn down the heat and simmer the sauce for 2–3 minutes, stirring occasionally. Pureé the cooked onions and add to the sauce. Season well. Set aside until ready to reheat for serving.

Remove the brisket from the saucepan and strain the stock, discarding vegetables and herbs. Replace the brisket and remaining stock in the pan and bring back to the boil. Turn down the heat so that the stock is gently simmering. You can now add the vegetables you wish to serve with the brisket such as neat chunks of carrot and turnip or the white part of a couple of leeks. When adding the vegetables bear in mind the length of time each one takes to cook, so that they are all ready at the same time.

Remove the brisket from the stock and place on a large serving dish surrounded by the vegetables. Serve with the onion sauce.

JP

Beef à la Will Moreland

I have a friend who is almost as talented a cook as he is a violinist, and I am most grateful to him for this recipe.

a 900g/2lb piece of fillet or sirloin of beef
2 tbsp oil
a bunch of spring onions, chopped
2 cloves of garlic, chopped
a piece of fresh root ginger the size of your thumb, chopped
1 tbsp soya sauce
a large bunch of fresh coriander, chopped
2 fresh chillies, chopped
a piece of lemon grass, roughly chopped
2 tins coconut milk
juice of 1 lime

Heat a heavy frying pan and seal your piece of meat thoroughly; remove. Heat the oil in the same pan and sauté the spring onions, garlic and ginger until softened. Add the soya sauce, half of the coriander and the chillies. The heat of the chillies is a matter of choice – you can use a Scots bonnet for ultra-hot or a deseeded jalapeño for mild. Decide before you buy.

Place the sealed meat in a roasting tin. Pour over the fried vegetable mixture. Add the lemon grass and pour the coconut milk and lime juice over the meat. Cook in a preheated oven at 180°C/350°F/Gas 4 for 40 minutes. Place the beef on a serving dish. Strain the sauce, add the rest of the chopped coriander and pour over the meat. Serve immediately.

CDW

Beef Stew with Prunes and Pumpkin Scones

Save British beef by eating more of it is what I say. This is a lovely rich comforting stew for the cold winter months. The Pumpkin Scones can be served with the stew or put on top as a cobbler.

900/2lb stewing beef, cubed
25g/1oz dripping
450g/1lb prunes, soaked
1 tbsp flour
300ml/½ pint beef stock

FOR THE MARINADE:
1 bottle red wine
4 tbsp olive oil
1 carrot, sliced
1 onion, sliced
2 cloves garlic, crushed
piece of orange peel
1 tsp juniper berries, crushed
pinch of nutmeg
2 sprigs thyme
2 bayleaves, crushed
6 black peppercorns, crushed
2 tbsp brandy (optional)

FOR THE PUMPKIN SCONES:
115g/4oz butter, softened
¼ tsp nutmeg
1 tsp salt
freshly ground black pepper
115g/4oz cooked mashed pumpkin
1 egg
120ml/4floz milk
750g/1½lb flour
1 tsp baking powder
milk to glaze

Place the meat in a large non-metallic bowl. Combine all the ingredients for the marinade, pour over the meat and refrigerate for 48 hours, turning occasionally. Strain, reserving the marinade, and wipe dry.

Brown the meat in the hot dripping. Transfer to a casserole and pour over the marinade. Cover and cook in a preheated oven at 150°C/300°F/Gas 2 for 2½ hours. Simmer the soaked prunes in a little salt water for 20–30 minutes or until soft. When the meat has finished cooking, remove from the oven and put on one side. Heat the oven to 220°C/425°F/Gas 7 for the scones.

To make the scones, combine butter, nutmeg, salt, pepper and pumpkin. Mix in the egg and add the milk, sift in flour and baking powder and mix to a soft dough. Turn onto a floured board and knead lightly. Roll to 2cm/¾ inch thick and cut into rounds using a small cup or pastry cutter. Place on a greased baking tray 1cm/½ inch apart and glaze with milk. Bake in the preheated oven for 15–20 minutes. Cool slightly before serving with the stew.

Reduce the meat's stew juices by rapid boiling. Mix the flour and the stock to a paste and blend into the juices and then push through a sieve with the vegetables. Return the meat and the prunes to the sauce and simmer gently on top of the stove for another 15 minutes.

CDW

Beef with Anchovies

In the Middle Ages, saltfish was cooked with meat, as it still is in the Caribbean. Anchovies were the great fashion in the Georgian Age so this is their adaptation of the earlier idea.

a 900g/2lb boned rib of beef
10 anchovy fillets
25g/1oz butter
2 carrots
1 onion
2 sticks of celery
450ml/¾ pint brown stock

Mash half of the anchovies with the butter, melt in a pan and brown the beef in it. Remove the meat and discard the butter. Using a larding needle or a sharp knife, make small holes in the meat and insert the remaining anchovies.

Finely chop the carrots, onion and celery and combine to make a mirepoix. Place the mirepoix of vegetables on the bottom of a heavy pan or casserole. Put the beef on top and pour over the stock. Bring to the boil, then cook gently for 1½ hours, uncovered. Cut into slices for serving.

CDW

Carpet Bag Steak

This is not really a carpet bag steak, it's a carpet bag roast. Redolent of an older age, maybe Dickensian, when huge steaks were eaten by gentlemen in their pubs and clubs. Curiously enough the oysters impart a very good flavour to the beef but do tell any guests in case they are allergic to the mollusc.

1.75kg/4lb piece of topside beef
55g/2oz butter
12–18 oysters, shelled
115g/4oz mushrooms, sliced
150g/6oz breadcrumbs
grated rind of a lemon
1 tbsp parsley
salt and paprika, to taste
1 egg, beaten

Ask the butcher to make a pocket in the topside.

Heat the butter in a frying pan, add the oysters and mushrooms and cook for about 5 minutes. Transfer to a basin, add the breadcrumbs, lemon rind, parsley, seasoning and beaten egg and mix thoroughly. Stuff the mixture into the pocket of the beef and skewer or sew the edges together. Roast in a preheated moderate oven 160°C/325°F/Gas 3 for 2 hours.

JP

Lamb Kebabs with Spiced Aubergine Sauce

If you are a barbecue addict this makes a change from charred raw sausages and salmonella. Just serve the aubergine sauce as a dip.

900g/2lb lamb, cut into bite-size pieces
4 large tomatoes, cut into quarters
12 medium-sized mushrooms, stalks removed, halved
1 yellow pepper, de-seeded and cut into strips

FOR THE MARINADE:
½ cup olive oil
juice of 1 lemon
1 clove of garlic, finely chopped
1 large onion, finely chopped
1 tsp cumin
½ tsp coriander
½ tsp salt
½ tsp ground black pepper

FOR THE AUBERGINE SAUCE:
900g/2lb aubergine
3 tbsp olive oil
2 cloves of garlic, chopped
1 tsp cumin
pinch of nutmeg
pinch of salt and freshly ground black pepper
juice of 1 lemon
1 tbsp chopped parsley

Combine the marinade ingredients. Marinate the lamb, tomatoes, mushrooms and yellow pepper for 2 hours or overnight. Skewer alternately lamb, tomatoes, mushrooms and yellow pepper.

Slice the aubergines, place in a pie dish and pour over the olive oil, sprinkle on the garlic, cumin, nutmeg, salt, pepper and lemon juice. Cook in a preheated hot oven at 200°C/400°F/Gas 6 for about 30 minutes. Remove from the oven and allow to cool, remove all the black skin and squeeze and discard the bitter juices out of the aubergines. Purée the flesh with the residue and pour into a saucepan.

Grill the kebabs, turning frequently. Heat the aubergine sauce, mix in the chopped parsley. Serve the sauce with the cooked kebabs.

JP

Oxford John

This is an excellent dish if you want the taste of leg of lamb or mutton, but for reasons of expense, quantity or time you don't want to buy the whole joint. In Scotland this particular cut has the splendid name 'giget chops'.

½ tsp each ground mace, dried thyme and chopped parsley
115g/4oz finely chopped onion
4 slices of lamb or mutton, cut from the leg (115g/4oz each)
55g/2oz butter
25g/1oz plain flour
450ml/¾ pint lamb stock
juice of 1 lemon
salt and freshly ground pepper

Mix together the mace, thyme, parsley and onion, and coat the lamb slices on both sides with this. Gently fry the meat in the butter for 10 minutes, turning once. Remove the meat and set aside. Stir the flour into the fat in the pan, add the stock and simmer for 5 minutes, stirring. Return the meat to the pan and add the lemon juice. Simmer for a further 5 minutes. Adjust seasoning and serve.

CDW

Lamb Couscous

A fine festive dish to set in the middle of a well crowded table. They present the whole sheep on a vast tray in the Middle East, eyes and all. Yum yum.

2 tbsp olive oil
2 medium onions, cut into thick slices
1 large clove of garlic, finely chopped
1½ tsp ground coriander
1½ tsp ground cumin
1 tsp ground cinnamon plus extra for sprinkling
½ tsp saffron strands
½ tsp ground ginger
3 tsp tomato purée
900g/2lb boneless leg of lamb, cubed
½ tsp harissa
salt and freshly ground pepper
115g/4oz dried chick peas, soaked overnight, or use ½ tin (adjust amount to to personal taste – I love chick peas)
2 large carrots, cut into chunks
2 small turnips, cut up
1 aubergine, cut into chunks
3 courgettes, cut into chunks
55g/2oz raisins
2 tomatoes, quartered
a large handful of chopped parsley
1 large handful of chopped fresh coriander
450g/1lb couscous

Heat the oil in a large saucepan, add the onions and cook for a few minutes to soften. Add the garlic, all the spices and the tomato purée and cook together for a few minutes, stirring. Add the cubed lamb and enough water (or stock if you have it) just to cover the lamb. Stir in ½ tsp of harissa (you can add more later on if you find it is not hot enough for you) and season with salt and pepper. Add the soaked dried chick peas. Bring to the boil, then simmer gently for about 30 minutes. Add the carrots and turnips, and cook for another 30 minutes before adding the aubergine, courgettes, raisins and tinned chick peas. After a further 20 minutes add the tomatoes and about half of the parsley and fresh coriander, keeping the remainder for the garnish. Check the seasoning and leave to cook for a further 5 minutes.

Meanwhile, prepare the couscous as instructed on the packet.

To serve, pile the couscous on a large serving dish and sprinkle with a little extra cinnamon. Arrange the meat and vegetables in the centre of the couscous, and sprinkle with the rest of the parsley and fresh coriander. Serve the broth in a separate bowl with smaller bowls for each person so that they can ladle out their own broth as a sauce, to which they can add extra harissa to their taste.

JP

Illustrated overleaf

Lancashire Hotpot

Whenever I read Dorothy Hartley's great book *Food in England* I become enraged by how deprived we are today to lose so much of our local identity. How far removed are the mushy burgers that are possibly poisoning us from the old local dishes and local breeds of animal. This dish was designed specially for the long-boned sheep of the Pennines, but I doubt you will find their long-tailed chops today. Ideally it should be made with mutton which has so much more flavour, but I expect you will have to make do with middle-aged hogget. Still, it is not a bad dish. A nice touch is to place a dozen fresh oysters under the potatoes.

2 mutton or lamb chops with their tail bones per person
plain flour
salt and freshly ground pepper
dripping or oil
1 lamb's kidney per person
1 onion per chop, sliced
4 carrots, sliced
potatoes, thickly sliced
1 tsp sugar

Trim the fat from your chops, dredge with flour and season. Fry them in hot dripping or oil till brown on both sides. Stand them vertically in a long casserole with the bones pointing upwards. Throw in the kidneys. Fry the onions lightly and pack among the chops, alternating with layers of sliced carrots. Arrange the potato slices on top, overlapping them to form a roof. Pour off the fat from the frying pan and make a gravy with a sprinkling of flour and boiling water. Season and add the sugar. Pour into the casserole, cover and cook in a preheated oven at 180°C/350°F/Gas 4 for 2 hours.

About 10 minutes before serving, remove the lid and allow the potatoes to brown. This dish is particularly good if made the day before and allowed to cool so that any surplus fat can be removed.

CDW

A.N.'s Slow Shoulder of Lamb

My beloved A.N. Wilson dreamt up this dish for the hurried cook who has to go out and about and likes to return to a fait accompli at the end of the day. He is a very good cook and deeply interested in food, but has little time to indulge. This receipt uses tins of haricot beans but you can of course cook your own if you prefer.

1 shoulder of lamb, about 1.8kg/4lb
2 large tins of haricot beans or 4 small ones
300–450ml/½–¾ pint white wine
2 large onions
10 shallots
6 tomatoes, quartered
3 tbsp tomato purée
salt and black peppercorns
10 whole cloves of garlic, peeled
2 bayleaves
3 branches of rosemary

Ask your butcher to cut off the knuckle end of the shoulder but keep it. (This makes it easier to fit in a casserole.) Put both pieces of the shoulder in a good ovenware pot. Cover with the beans and their liquid, the wine, onions and shallots roughly chopped, the tomatoes and the purée, the garlic, several crushed peppercorns and salt to taste. Tuck in the bayleaves and the rosemary. A.N. has an Aga and cooks the shoulder for about 4 hours in the simmering oven and then in the roasting oven for another hour or so to suit himself. With an ordinary cooker, I would put the covered casserole in a preheated oven at 140°C/275°F/Gas 1 for the 4 hours, then increase the temperature to 220°C/425°F/Gas 7 for the last part. Have a look at it now and then to make sure it is not drying out; also give it the odd stir to combine all the vegetables and juices.

The first 4 hours can be done the day before and is really no trouble. I would also add some anchovies, which are excellent with lamb; you cannot actually taste them but they have a very enhancing effect on the flavour. Black olives are another good addition. At the end of cooking, the meat will drop off the bone and all the fat will have disappeared into the vegetables in some miraculous manner. Serve in good, big old-fashioned soup plates. For accompaniment this dish requires nothing more than a vast, crisp green salad and a good crust of bread.

JP

Harrira

This middle eastern, somewhat peasant, stew is a useful and comforting supper dish which is also good for using up the leftovers from a leg of lamb instead of buying fresh meat should you so desire. Waste not want not.

115g/4oz chickpeas
350/¾ lb lamb, cubed into bite-size pieces
1 large onion, chopped
1 tbsp olive oil
25g/1oz butter
1 tsp ground ginger
1 tsp coriander
1 tsp turmeric
¼ tsp cayenne
¼ tsp cinnamon
salt and freshly ground pepper
900ml–1.2 litres/1½–2 pints chicken stock
400g/14oz chopped, or tinned, tomatoes
55g/2oz long grain rice
pinch of saffron
1 red pepper, skinned, de-seeded and cut in strips
juice of 1 lemon
1 tbsp chopped parsley

Soak the chickpeas overnight, drain and cook rapidly for 10 minutes and then simmer for a further 20 minutes and then drain. Fry the onion in oil and butter until translucent, add the cubed lamb and brown evenly. Add the ginger, coriander, turmeric, cayenne, cinnamon, salt and pepper to taste and fry for a few minutes.

Transfer to a saucepan in which you have the chicken stock, cover and cook gently for an hour. Add the chick peas, tomatoes, rice, red pepper and lemon juice, and cook for a further 30 minutes. Sprinkle with chopped parsley before serving.

JP

Pork Stroganoff

This is a steal from the famous Russian dish. I have used gin in the sauce as I usually do with pork – the juniper flavour of gin goes admirably with the meat. The alcohol content evaporates so it can be served at the most temperate of gatherings.

a 800g/1¾lb fillet of pork (approx)
1 tbsp olive oil
25g/1oz butter
2 onions, thinly sliced
225g/8oz mushrooms, thinly sliced
salt and freshly ground black pepper
2 tbsp gin
300ml/½ pint sour cream
chopped parsley
paprika

Remove any unsightly fat or outer skin from the pork. Slice across the grain into rounds about 5mm/¼in thick. Heat half the oil and butter in a large frying pan until sizzling. Fry half the pork briskly to brown on both sides, about 3 minutes. Transfer to a plate with a slotted spoon. Cook the other half of the pork ditto.

Add the rest of the butter and oil to the pan and cook the onions gently until soft, then add the mushrooms and continue to cook gently, turning them over and over until the juices run. Season with a little salt and lots of pepper. Remove the pan contents to another plate.

Reinstate the pork rounds in the pan, heat gently and pour the gin over the meat. Let it warm up for 2 minutes, then set fire to it and baste until the flames die out. Add the onions and mushrooms, stir in the sour cream and bring to a bubbling simmer. Check seasoning. Sprinkle with chopped parsley and a goodly pinch of paprika. Serve immediately with buttered noodles or plain boiled rice.

JP

Pork with Clams

That well-known dish that children love – Pork with Clams! As cooked for the Cotswold Hunt Pony Club, who relished the Portuguese import.

750g/1½lb pork loin
4 cloves of garlic
2 tsp salt
2 tbsp chilli sauce
4 tbsp lard
900g/2lb clams

Mix garlic and salt and crush into a paste. Brush the meat with the paste, then chilli sauce, cover and refrigerate for 24 hours. Cut the meat into squares. Wash the clams thoroughly in several changes of water. Fry the meat in the lard for 10 minutes, or until brown. Add the clams and cook over a high heat so they open quickly, discard any that do not open. Serve at once.

CDW

Illustrated overleaf

Pot-roasted Pork with Caraway

This is another Elizabethan recipe. In Scotland, where I live, loin of pork is not sold with its crackling, so I have found myself looking for recipes for other cuts. Shoulder is good and less expensive than loin.

a 1.8kg/4lb boned shoulder of pork
2 tbsp oil or lard
2 onions, sliced
2 tbsp caraway seeds
4 apples (sharp but not cookers), sliced
salt and freshly ground pepper
6 dates, pitted and halved
a piece of candied peel, chopped
1 head of celery, chopped
grated rind and juice of 1 orange
a sprig of fresh sage
½ bottle of red wine
brown stock

Heat the oil or lard in a frying pan and brown the joint of pork over a high heat, turning to colour all sides. Remove. Fry the onions in the same fat to a light brown. Add the caraway seeds and let them start to pop.

Put the onion and caraway mixture into a deep ovenproof dish or casserole. Layer the sliced apples on top. Season the pork and place on this mixture. Add the dates, candied peel, celery, orange rind and sage. Pour on the wine and orange juice and top up with enough stock to come to the top of but not cover the meat. Cook in a preheated oven at 170°C/325°F/Gas 3 for 2½ hours.

Remove the meat. Strain the cooking liquid and remove the fat from the surface. Serve the liquid as a sauce.

CDW

Pork Chops Marinated in Yoghurt and Dill

I bought the carcasses of a couple of two-year-old organically raised Tamworth pigs. They were the size of the sides of Highland beef they were hanging next to in my butchers and quite delicious. But it means I have been collecting a few pork recipes. This is a good and easy way of doing chops.

4 pork chops
2 tbsp chilli sauce
225g/8oz Greek yoghurt
3 tbsp chopped dill
oil
salt
coarsely crushed peppercorns

Mix the chilli, yoghurt and dill together, spread over the pork chops and place in a plastic bag. Leave to marinate for 3–24 hours. Remove the chops from the marinade and pat dry. Brush with oil, sprinkle with salt and the crushed peppercorns and cook either under the grill or on a griddle. I gently heat the marinade and serve it with the chops.

CDW

Loin of Pork Stuffed with Ceps or Truffles

Thsi is a wonderful dish to be eaten either hot or cold. In Périgord it is made with black truffles, and if you happen to have a small jar they are the ideal. Otherwise a very good flavour is achieved by using the Italian dried ceps, or funghi porcini secchi. What is most important is that the pork should be first class, from a proper butcher who deals with well-bred pigs and not those water-injected tasteless creatures.

a 1.8kg/4lb loin of pork
salt and freshly ground pepper
3 truffles or about 50g/2oz
dried ceps (porcini)
cloves of garlic, thinly sliced
450ml/¾ pint hot meat stock
or water
150ml/¼ pint white wine

Ask your butcher to bone the loin and remove the rind, but keep both bones and rind for the cooking. If you are using dried ceps, cover them with warm water and leave to soak for 30 minutes or so until they are soft. Drain, reserving the liquid. Lay the meat on a board and season well with salt and pepper. Cut the truffles or ceps into little pieces and lay at intervals along the meat interspersed with slivers of garlic. Roll the meat up and tie it with string into a long bolster shape. Place it in a roasting tin surrounded by the bones and the rind cut into strips. Roast in a preheated oven at 170°C/325°F/Gas 3 for 30 minutes. Pour in the hot stock or water, the wine and the liquid from soaking the ceps. Cover the tin and cook for a further 2–2½ hours.

Remove the pork and keep hot. Strain the juices and reduce, then season to taste. Serve with the sliced pork. Or, if serving the pork cold, pour off the juices into a bowl and chill. Remove the fat, but keep it for frying bread or little potatoes – it has a splendid flavour. The juices will have jellied and should be chopped and arranged around the cold pork in a serving dish. Serve with what you will, such as a fine salad and some sautéed potatoes.

JP

Ham with Pea Sauce

I love the combination of ham and peas. Be very careful when cooking your ham to ensure that the bubbles do not break the surface while it is simmering or the meat will toughen. My late brother and I spent many happy and inebriated hours watching our ham. I only hope someone cooks the ham for my funeral as painstakingly and lovingly as I did for his.

900g–1.5kg/2–3lb piece of ham or gammon, with rind removed
600ml/1 pint vegetable stock
300ml/½ pint white wine
2 potatoes, peeled and cubed
1 carrot, cubed
1 parsnip, peeled and cubed
1 onion, finely chopped
150ml/¼ pint sour cream
450g/1lb fresh peas or small packet frozen peas
salt and freshly ground pepper
1 tbsp butter

Simmer the ham in the stock and white wine for 40–60 minutes (allow 20 minutes per pound). Top up with water if the ham is not completely covered. Remove from the stock and keep warm. Cook the vegetables in the stock for about 5 minutes, strain and remove from the pan. Boil the stock fiercely to reduce to about 175ml/6fl oz (about half). Add sour cream and peas and heat through. Purée in a blender, or sieve and season. Reheat the sauce gently, do not let it come to the boil. Sauté the drained root vegetables in a little butter. Slice the meat thinly and serve with vegetables and sauce.

CDW

POULTRY AND GAME

Lock up your peacocks when Clarissa's around

One of the great mysteries of life is why so many people refuse to eat beef because of the BSE scare, which at worst (if you believe it and if you eat cheap beef) promises a one in six million risk, and prefer to eat chicken, which carries a high risk of salmonella. 'Oh,' you may say 'but I buy those free-range chickens the supermarkets offer'. However although these may taste better, the problem lies with the modern breeds, the speed with which they are raised and what they are fed on. Five weeks from egg to table is a terrifying thought and the flesh is loose on the bones, allowing disease to proliferate. The reason free-range chickens taste better rests in what they are fed, although they do not have much time to acquire any real flavour. The answer is to buy organically produced chickens of old breeds: then and only then will you know what chicken should taste like.

Other poultry is a different matter. Ducks and geese are not raised on such a large commercial scale so they tend to be better reared and have more flavour. Turkey, of course, is a breed apart. Even the most organically reared Bronze has not got a lot of flavour and the commercial ones have none at all.

How pleasant is a pheasant you have shot yourself

What I really like is the game in this chapter. I love all game and thank heavens the hunting laws, our legacy from William the Conqueror, ensure that it is still seasonal. You can now buy game in the supermarket, and this has the advantage of being prepared in amorphous little packages bearing little resemblance to the original creature. However, as Jennifer – who will shop in such places – points out, it is very seldom properly hung. Whilst very few people nowadays want to hang game until the head falls off, it is necessary to let it hang for a few days to a week in order to enhance the flavour and to tenderise it in the same way as meat. Another disadvantage of supermarket game is that it can be overpriced.

Farmed venison has the advantage of being consistently tender and young, but to my mind it does not have the flavour of the wild. Still, farmed venison is easier to cook, and you have to be careful when choosing wild meat – it is essential to use a good butcher. Pigeons, which are vermin, are not eaten nearly enough. And as for rabbit, Jennifer makes the point that people have been turned against rabbit because they ate it badly cooked as children or because of the horror of myxomatosis. It is time to set aside these prejudices. Rabbit is cheap, plentiful and delicious. If more were eaten the price would drop further. At the moment tons are shot and left to lie as keepers don't find a big enough market to make them worth collecting. Grouse and partridge are luxuries but worth buying as a treat.

Whatever poultry you buy, try to buy the best flavour and remember that although a proper organically raised chicken may be more expensive, it will go a lot further. When buying game go to a proper butcher, and remember that a young bird's beak and feet are relatively soft and pliable whilst horney old claws are a sign to casserole the creature or put it in a pie.

Taking a break from all that cooking

Lemon and Saffron Chicken

Saffron is one of the most expensive spices there is, but you need very little and the flavour it produces is well worth the price.

a good pinch of saffron threads
2 tbsp hot water
1 medium sized chicken, jointed (preferably free range)
55g/2oz butter
1 tbsp oil
1 onion, sliced
1 large carrot, cut into finger-length chunks
3 sticks of celery, sliced
300ml/½ pint good chicken stock
juice of ½ a lemon
white wine
salt and freshly ground pepper

FOR THE SAUCE:
40g/1½oz butter
40g/1½oz plain flour
450ml/¾ pint stock (from the chicken)
150ml/¼ pint double cream
2 egg yolks
grated rind of 1 lemon
115g/4oz mushrooms, sliced and sautéed in butter
chopped fresh coriander
salt and freshly ground pepper
lemon juice (optional)

Fry the saffron threads in a dry frying pan for a few minutes, then soak in the hot water for 15 minutes. Melt the butter with the oil in the frying pan and fry the chicken joints until they change colour. Lay the chicken joints on top of the sliced onions, carrots and celery in a casserole dish. Add the chicken stock, lemon juice, a generous dash of white wine and the saffron liquid, and season with salt and pepper. Cook in a preheated oven at 200°C/400°F/Gas 6 for 1¼–1½ hours. Remove the chicken joints, carrots and celery and keep warm. Strain the cooking liquid into a saucepan. Add a small glass of white wine and boil rapidly for a few minutes to reduce to 450ml/¾ pint. Reserve for the sauce

To make the sauce, melt the butter in a saucepan, add the flour and blend with the butter. Slowly add the reserved chicken stock and cook, stirring constantly, over a low heat until it comes to the boil. Simmer sauce gently, stirring occasionally, for 5–10 minutes.

Beat egg yolks, cream and lemon rind together.

Remove sauce from heat and stir in the egg mixture. Season with salt and pepper and add mushrooms and chopped fresh coriander to taste. Add a little more lemon juice if necessary.

JP

Chicken Simla

Shades of the British memsahibs reclining in Simla. If you prefer, use a good curry paste which you can buy either hot or medium according to your taste. Though not a true Indian receipt this is surprisingly good and can be eaten either hot or cold.

1.5kg/3lb chicken jointed
85g/3oz butter
1 medium onion, chopped
1 stick celery, chopped into 2.5cm/1in pieces
1 sprig parsley
1 sprig fresh thyme
1 bayleaf
salt and freshly ground pepper
1 clove of garlic, crushed
2 tsp curry powder
pinch of saffron
300ml/½ pint Béchamel sauce
120ml/¼ pint coconut milk
120ml/¼ pint single cream
juice of 1 lemon

Melt the butter and gently fry the chicken joints and onion until the joints are a pale golden colour, do not allow to brown. Lay the celery, parsley, thyme and bayleaf in a casserole, place the chicken joints on top and sprinkle over the salt and pepper, crushed garlic, curry powder and cooked onions. Cook in a preheated moderate oven 180°C/350°F/Gas 4 for 35–40 minutes until the chicken is cooked but not brown. Remove the chicken, put it in a clean casserole and replace in the oven to cook for a further 20 minutes while you prepare the sauce.

Infuse the saffron in 2 tablespoons of water.

To the remaining casserole add the Béchamel sauce and coconut milk, mix to take up all the chicken juices and transfer to a saucepan. Bring the sauce to the boil and simmer gently for about 20 minutes – stirring frequently. Strain into another saucepan, add the cream and reheat – you may add a little more coconut milk if the consistency is not quite right. Strain the infused saffron water and add to the sauce with the lemon juice. Pour the sauce over the chicken and serve.

JP

Calcutta Chicken Croquettes

My maternal grandfather died young of the demon drink, leaving my grandmother with two young children. Fortunately she met my step-grandfather, an extremely wealthy Sephardic Jew from Calcutta. For years she refused to marry him because he was a Jew and she was a Catholic. They lived together in great luxury with sixty indoor servants in what is now the British Residency in Singapore. I was reminded of this excellent dish by Claudia Roden's brilliant *Book of Jewish Food* and dug out my step-great grandmother's version.

225g/8 oz cold basmati rice (cook and drain but don't rinse, to leave in the starch)
450g/1lb finely minced chicken
2 onions, finely chopped
5–7.5cm/2–3in piece of ginger, grated
1 tsp garam masala
½ tsp turmeric
1 bunch coriander, finely chopped
1 bunch flat parsley, finely chopped
4 tbsp chicken fat or vegetable oil for frying

In a large bowl mix all the ingredients except the chicken fat or oil. If the rice is not sticky enough you can add an egg to bind. This can be done in a food processor but I feel the resulting mixture doesn't have enough texture. Form into 5cm/2in croquettes and fry in the hot chicken fat or oil until deep gold.

CDW

Wylde Green Chicken

Commonly known as Wild Green Chicken. This is a dish I invented when staying with Christine, my best friend from school, who lives in Wylde Green Road in Birmingham. It is a dish designed to deal with the problem of tasteless chicken, and it proved so popular with my godchildren that I had to write it down.

6 chicken breasts
2 tbsp crunchy peanut butter
2 cloves of garlic, finely chopped
2 tbsp olive oil
1 tsp dried mustard
1 tsp paprika
1 tsp each salt and freshly ground pepper
1 tsp chilli sauce
1 tbsp dark rum or wine vinegar
300ml/½ pint water

Mix together the peanut butter, garlic and half the oil. Lay the chicken breasts in a dish, pour the mixture over them, turn and work well into the meat. Leave to stand for at least 30 minutes. In a large frying pan heat the rest of the oil and dissolve the mustard, paprika, salt and pepper into it. Tip the chicken breasts with the marinade into the pan and sauté until they are coloured. At this stage I usually cut them into pieces in the pan. Add the chilli sauce, the rum and the water and cook over a low heat until they are cooked through, usually about 10 minutes. Serve with new potatoes or rice and a green salad.

CDW

Poussin with Garlic

I first made this dish with smoked garlic, which I found in my local market; however, it is not readily available so use the natural. A good mixture of tastes from the four corners of the earth.

2 poussins
black olive paste
lemon juice
6 tbsp olive oil
10 plump cloves of garlic
150ml/¼ pint dry vermouth
sea salt and freshly ground pepper
bayleaves
black bean sauce

Take a small flameproof casserole that will fit the birds snugly. Put a tbsp of olive paste and a good squeeze of lemon into each cavity. Heat the olive oil in the casserole and brown the poussins all over, turning from side to side. Add the peeled cloves of garlic and allow to cook gently for a minute or two. Pour in the vermouth (Sainsbury's Italian has a good flavour and is reasonable). Season well with salt and pepper, and tuck in a couple of bayleaves. Brush the birds liberally with some black bean sauce.

Cover the casserole with its lid and cook in a preheated oven at 190°C/375°F/Gas 5 for about 45 minutes until tender. Baste every 15 minutes. Good served with rice.

JP

Coq au Vin

Do not be dismayed at the colour of this sauce, which is rather dingy. It's meant to look like that. If your chicken is not a real free range bird you can reduce the cooking time. Take care not to over cook, which will result in the meat shredding.

1 bottle of red wine
a few sprigs of fresh thyme
2 bayleaves
a few sprigs of parsley
1 medium-sized chicken, jointed (use free range for more flavour)
1 tbsp vegetable oil
115g/4oz streaky bacon, cut into strips or lardoons
2 onions, chopped
plain flour
1 glass of brandy
2 cloves of garlic, chopped
115g/4oz mushrooms, halved or quartered if large
20 small button onions
55g/2oz butter
2 tsp sugar
beurre manié, made with 1 tsp each plain flour and butter mixed to a paste
1 tbsp chopped parsley

Bring the red wine to the boil with the sprigs of thyme and parsley and the bayleaves, then leave to cool for 1 hour. Pour the wine over the jointed chicken and marinate for 12 hours.

Fry the streaky bacon in a frying pan; remove with a slotted spoon. Add the oil to the pan and fry the onions until softened. Remove the chicken joints from the marinade and pat dry with kitchen paper. Dust the chicken joints with a little flour, then put them in the frying pan and brown them lightly. Pour in the warmed brandy and flambé it. Transfer the chicken joints and liquid to a casserole and add the bacon, strained marinade, garlic and mushrooms. Cover and cook in a preheated oven at 150°C/300°F/Gas 2 for about 1 hour.

In the meantime, fry the small onions in butter with the sugar and a little water until glazed. Add to the casserole and cook for a further 30 minutes. If the sauce needs thickening, stir in a few small knobs of beurre manié. Remove casserole from the oven and sprinkle the chopped parsley over before serving.

JP

Oriental Chicken Pudding

This looks magnificent when presented steaming at the table – full of different flavours and good for lunch on a cold winter's day. You could use suet instead of butter in the pastry. Great for hungry boys.

900g/2lb boned chicken breast cut into chunks
25g/1oz plain flour
salt and freshly ground black pepper
olive oil
3 heads chicory
2 tbsp freshly chopped coriander
1 bunch spring onions, chopped
2 large cloves of garlic
coarsely grated rind and juice of 1 lemon
1 tbsp soya sauce
5cm/2in piece of fresh ginger, grated

FOR THE PASTRY:
150g/6oz self-raising flour
3 tsp paprika
1 tsp ground mace
2 tsp paprika
2 tsp chervil
3–4 pinches cayenne pepper
115g/4oz fresh white breadcrumbs
150g/6oz frozen butter
1 egg

Coat the chicken pieces with the plain flour seasoned with salt and pepper. Heat the olive oil in a heavy-bottomed pan over a high heat. Add the chicken pieces and brown on all sides and then leave on one side to cool.

Mix together the self-raising flour, spices, breadcrumbs, chervil, cayenne pepper and salt to taste in a bowl. Hold the butter in a damp cloth at one end and grate it into the mixture, mixing it with your hands. Whisk the egg in a measuring jug and top it up with water to a total of 1.75ml/6fl oz. Gradually mix the liquid into the flour and butter. Bring it together and form a ball. Save a quarter of the dough for a lid. Roll out the rest of the dough fairly thinly into a circle with a diameter of about 35cm/14in. Line a 1.75-litre/3-pint pudding basin with the pastry leaving the edges to overlap the top of the basin. Don't worry if the pastry breaks, just gently patch it together with your hand.

Cut the chicory into thick slices and mix with the coriander, spring onions, garlic, chicken, lemon rind and soya sauce. Add the lemon juice and season. Spoon this mixture into the basin so that it forms a mound at the top. Fold the pastry over the filling and wet the edges. Roll out the saved dough into a circle big enough to form the top. Seal the edges by pressing them lightly. Take a buttered piece of greaseproof paper and make a pleat in the middle before putting it over the top of the pudding. Put a piece of foil loosely over the paper and tie both securely with string. Make a handle with string and lower the pudding into a saucepan of boiling water. Cover and boil gently for 3 hours, check the water level at regular intervals and top up as required.

JP

Chicken with Red Pepper Sauce

It is always useful to have different ways to prepare chicken, fast becoming the staple food in many a household. Do try to get a chicken which has run naked and unencumbered throughout its formative years – otherwise known as free range. It really does make all the difference and the bones make wonderful stock.

1.5kg/3lb chicken, jointed
55g/2oz butter
2 tbsp vegetable oil
6 small shallots
2 red peppers, de-seeded
2 cloves of garlic
150ml/¼ pint white wine
salt and freshly ground pepper
1 tsp dried oregano
1 tbsp tomato purée
1 tbsp chopped parsley

Melt the butter with the vegetable oil and add the shallots, red peppers and garlic. Fry gently until the shallots and pepper are just soft. Remove with a slotted spoon and set aside. Turn up the heat and fry the chicken joints on both sides. Put the chicken joints in a casserole dish, spoon the peppers and shallots on top, pour in the wine, add 1 teaspoon salt and ½ teaspoon pepper and the oregano. Cook in a preheated medium oven at 190°C/375°F/Gas 5 for 45–55 minutes. Remove the chicken joints and pour the liquid with the peppers, shallots and garlic into a liquidiser. Add the parsley and liquidise. Pour the sauce over the chicken joints and serve.

JP

Steamroller Chicken

This is a Peshwari dish, so named because the chickens are spatchcocked and flattened to look as if they have been run over by a steamroller.

2 small chickens
4 tbsp ghee

FOR THE PASTE:
1 onion, chopped
a 2.5cm/1in piece of fresh root
ginger, chopped
3 tbsp ghee
1 tbsp ground coriander
1½ tsp ground cumin
1 tsp turmeric
1 tsp cayenne pepper
½ tsp ground cardamom
¼ tsp ground cloves
¼ tsp ground cinnamon
2 cloves of garlic, smashed
juice of 1 lemon

Combine all the ingredients for the paste in a food processor, and process to a fine texture. Halve the chickens lengthways and whack them hard with the flat of a cleaver until they are flattened. Rub the chickens all over with the paste and put in a bowl with the remainder of the paste. Cover and leave in the fridge overnight.

Grill the chickens under a preheated hot grill for 10 minutes on each side, basting with both the marinade and the ghee. Serve with naan bread and chutneys.

CDW

Turkey Vendageuse

It seems strange to think of French grape pickers eating turkey, but this recipe, found in a strange old book called *Customs in the Perigord and Quercy*, seems to suggest otherwise. I was not really a fan of turkey until one Christmas, when I ordered a real free-range bird from the Chatsworth farm shop at the advice of my friend, the food expert Henrietta Green. The taste and texture of the turkey was so different that I was converted. However, even with the rather flaccid examples on supermarket shelves, this is a good dish.

SERVES 6

3 turkey breasts
3 cloves of garlic, cut into slivers
2 rashers of unsmoked streaky bacon, cut into short, thin strips
1 tbsp pork, goose or duck fat
1 onion, sliced
1 carrot, sliced
6 cloves
1 bouquet garni
300ml/½ pint chicken stock
salt and freshly ground pepper
1 tbsp cognac
6 artichoke hearts, cooked
225g/8oz green grapes, deseeded (unless seedless)

Flatten the turkey breasts and cut them in half lengthways so that you have 6 fillets. Remove any skin. Make small slits all over the turkey fillets and stick in the slivers of garlic and bacon. Smear the fat over the bottom of a shallow flameproof casserole, and scatter in the onion and carrot. Put the turkey fillets on top and add the cloves and bouquet garni. Add the stock and season with salt and pepper. Cook in a preheated oven at 180°C/350°F/Gas 4 for 25 minutes, basting frequently; the turkey fillets should be cooked through but moist and tender.

Transfer the turkey to a hot dish and keep warm. Skim off the excess fat from the cooking liquid in the pan and deglaze with the cognac, stirring well. Add the artichoke hearts and grapes, and reduce the sauce by boiling fiercely for a couple of minutes. Surround the turkey fillets with the artichoke hearts and grapes. Strain the sauce and spoon over the meat.

CDW

Turkey Pilaff in Filo Pastry

I am not a great fan of turkey but I am always being asked for ways of using it and there is no doubt that if you cook one there will be leftovers. A pilaff is a Persian dish and enclosed in filo pastry this has quite a Turkish flavour, even if the name of the bird is merely a historical mistake.

150g/6oz butter
1 onion, finely chopped
55g/2oz pine nuts
225g/8oz long grain rice
600ml/1 pint chicken stock
2 tomatoes
2 tbsp currants
½ tsp allspice
pinch of nutmeg
½ tsp sugar
½ tsp cayenne
salt and freshly ground pepper
½ red pepper, chopped
1 stick celery, chopped
1 small courgette, chopped
4 chicken livers, chopped
225g/8oz turkey raw or cooked, sliced in thin strips
juice and rind of 1 lemon
8 sheets filo pastry
melted butter

In a large pan heat 115g/4oz of the butter and cook the onion until soft, add pine nuts and rice and cook over heat until slightly coloured. Add half the chicken stock a little at a time to allow the rice to absorb it. Stir in the tomatoes, currants, spices, sugar and seasoning. Pour on the rest of the chicken stock and bring to the boil, reduce the heat, cover and simmer until the rice is tender and the stock is absorbed, about 15–20 minutes.

In a small pan heat the remaining butter and sauté the pepper, celery and courgette. Add the chicken livers and turkey strips if uncooked, season and cook until the chicken livers are just done. Add this to the rice mixture with lemon juice and rind. Grease an 20cm/8in cake tin. Brush each sheet of filo with melted butter. Place sheets to cover inside of tin, letting them hang over the sides. Fill with the mixture, fold pastry over the top and brush with melted butter. Bake at 180°C/350°F/Gas 4 for 25–30 minutes until golden brown. Turn onto a dish and serve hot or cold.

CDW

Duck in Honey Sauce

I remember my mother cooking duck, which she rubbed enthusiastically with salt and honey. The duck was so good that Boris Chaliapin, the son of the great opera singer, espying one left over at the end of the lunch, devoured the lot by way of a savoury. For my mother's method roast at 180°C/350°F/Gas 4 for 2 hours. This is a variant on the idea.

4 duck breasts
115g/4oz butter
2 tbsp olive oil
1 onion, finely chopped
85ml/3fl oz white wine
85g/3oz honey
2 sprigs of fresh thyme
juice of 1 lemon
600ml/1 pint double cream
salt and freshly ground pepper

Cut each duck breast into two. Heat 55g/2oz butter with the oil in a frying pan and fry the pieces of duck without allowing them to colour. Add the onion and allow to soften. Remove the duck from the pan and keep warm. Pour off any excess fat.

Add the wine to the pan and boil to reduce slightly. Stir in the honey and thyme. Add the lemon juice and cream, and season with salt and pepper. Replace the duck in the pan; cover and cook for a further 5 minutes.

Remove the duck to a serving dish. Discard the thyme and swirl the remaining butter, in small pieces, into the sauce. Pour over the duck and garnish with fresh thyme.

CDW

Duck in Red Wine Sauce

This is a useful dish to prepare in advance if you are a working person. Just heat it up before you need to eat it. The flavours intensify, as with many a casserole dish, on reheating.

1.75kg/4lb duck, jointed
salt and freshly ground pepper
25g/1oz plain flour
55g/2oz butter
2 tbsp olive oil
55g/2oz chopped shallots
115g/4oz bacon lardons
300ml/½ pint red wine
6 crushed peppercorns
1 bayleaf
600ml/1 pint chicken stock
16 whole button onions
225g/8oz mushrooms, sliced
1 tsp sugar

FOR THE BEURRE MANIE:
40g/1½ oz butter
25g/1oz flour

Sprinkle duck joints with salt, pepper and flour and sauté in 25g/1oz melted butter and 1 tablespoon of oil until golden brown. Place duck joints in casserole dish. Cook the shallots and lardons in the oil and butter for a few minutes. Add the wine, peppercorns and bayleaf. Boil to reduce to half, then add the stock and again reduce by half. Strain sauce over duck and cook gently in a pre-heated oven at 190°C/375°F/Gas 5, for 1 hour but check to make sure the duck joints are cooked.

Meanwhile melt the remaining butter and oil in the frying pan, add the button onions, sprinkle with sugar and brown. After the duck has been cooking for 30 minutes add the onions and the raw mushrooms. When the duck joints are cooked, set to one side, check the sauce for consistency and seasoning and, if necessary, thicken with the *beurre manié*. To make this, knead the butter and flour together and form into a small knob.

JP

Guinea Fowl

I remember cooking this after Mass at the London Oratory, which was fraught with excitement after a mad woman had stalked up to the altar and emptied a carrier bag full of rubbish on the steps, old dog food tins and milk cartons for the most part. She was yelling in some foreign tongue and had to be led away.

1 guinea fowl
85g/3oz salt pork or streaky bacon, diced
115g/4oz shallots, chopped
olive oil
the bird's liver or chicken liver, chopped
85g/3oz stoned black olives, chopped
1 tbsp fresh thyme leaves

Fry the diced pork or bacon and the shallots in about 3 tbsp of olive oil until they are beginning to brown. Add the liver and stir-fry for a minute. Add the olives and thyme and mix well together. Remove from the heat and stuff into the bird's cavity. Brush the bird all over with olive oil, place in a snug baking tin and cook in a pre-heated oven at 220°C/425°F/Gas 7 for an hour. Baste well every 20 minutes or so while you are enjoying your pre-prandial cocktails.

Serve with nice little potatoes and some juicy sautéed endive, which goes very well with a bird. By endive I mean the white bomb-shaped creatures which are sometimes called chicory.

JP

Guinea Fowl with Jerusalem Artichokes, Mushrooms and Button Onions

For those who are a little faint of heart and do not like the strong flavour of a well-hung pheasant, this provides an ideal alternative. Guinea fowl can be dry, but this receipt works a treat every time.

1 large plump guinea fowl, or
2 small ones
1 tbsp oil
115g/4oz butter
4 shallots, finely chopped
1 clove of garlic
225g/½lb mushrooms, sliced
450g/1lb Jerusalem artichokes
16 button onions
150ml/¼ pint single cream
2 egg yolks
salt and freshly ground pepper
1 tbsp chopped parsley

Brown the guinea fowl in the oil and half the butter in a large frying pan and put in a casserole. Fry the shallots and garlic and add to the casserole. Cook the guinea fowl in a preheated moderate oven at 190°C/375°F/Gas 5 for 1 hour.

In the meantime, fry the mushrooms gently for 2–3 minutes. Cut the artichokes into fairly uniform pieces. Parboil the button onions and artichokes for no more than 5 minutes and strain. Add the mushrooms, button onions and artichokes to the casserole and cook for a further 30 minutes. Remove casserole from the oven, pour heated sherry over the fowl and ignite. Remove the fowl and joint it, arrange on a serving dish with the vegetables around it and keep it warm.

Stir the cream into the juices remaining in the casserole with a wooden spoon, then pour into a saucepan and boil rapidly to reduce. Remove from the heat and stir in the beaten egg yolks with salt and pepper to taste. Pour a little sauce over the guinea fowl and sprinkle over the chopped parsley. Serve the remainder of the sauce in a sauceboat.

JP

Cream Smothered Pheasant

For people with an endless supply of the little creatures, another way to enjoy pheasant.

1 large or 2 small pheasants
1 tbsp vegetable oil
85g/3oz butter
1 medium onion
2 cloves of garlic
600ml/1 pint white wine
300ml/½ pint stock, made
from giblets minus liver
bouquet garni of parsley,
bayleaf and thyme
pinch of nutmeg
salt and freshly ground pepper
25g/1oz flour
300ml/½ pint double cream
3 egg yolks, beaten
1 tbsp chopped parsley

Sauté the pheasant in the oil and 55g/2oz butter in a frying pan until golden brown all over. Put the pheasant in a casserole. Fry the onion and garlic in the pan but do not brown. Add the wine, stock, bouquet garni, nutmeg, salt and pepper and bring to the boil, then pour over the pheasant. Cook in a preheated medium oven at 200°C/400°F/Gas 6 until the pheasant is tender, about 1–1½ hours. Transfer the pheasant to the serving dish and keep warm. Boil the casserole juices in a saucepan to reduce by half.

Melt the remaining butter in a saucepan, add the flour, stir and cook for a few minutes. Gradually add the pan juices, stirring constantly, then add the cream. Lower the heat and simmer for a few minutes. Remove the saucepan from the heat and stir in the beaten egg yolks. Test for seasoning and sprinkle with parsley. Pour a little over the pheasant and serve the remainder in a sauceboat.

JP

Pheasant with Chestnuts in Pastry

When I worked on the pheasant farm in Sussex I learnt to sympathise with those who have endless pheasants to cook and spent a lot of time thinking up recipes. I particularly like this one because it is so good for a dinner party. You can get to the stage where you wrap the pheasant earlier in the day and just bung it in the oven at the relevant time, and the pastry stops it drying out. It's also a good recipe for guinea fowl and chicken.

1 pheasant
450g/1lb chestnuts
85g/3oz butter
225g/8oz pheasant or chicken livers, chopped
225g/8oz bacon, minced
2 onions, chopped
salt and freshly ground pepper
300ml/½ pint game or chicken stock
350g/12oz puff pastry
1 egg yolk, beaten

FOR THE SHERRY SAUCE:
55g/2oz butter
55g/2oz flour
750ml/1¼ pints chicken stock
salt and pepper
50ml/3tbsp double cream
30g/1oz butter
50ml/3tbsp dry sherry

Peel the chestnuts and simmer in salted water until tender but still whole. Mix together the bacon, livers, chestnuts, onion and 25g/1oz of the butter, and seasoning. Stuff the pheasant with the mixture. Brown the pheasant in the rest of the butter add the stock and roast in a preheated oven at 200°C/400°F/Gas 6 for 20 minutes, turning onto the other side half way through. Baste frequently. Remove from the oven and allow to cool. Roll the pastry out and wrap the bird in it. Cut a slit for steam and brush with the egg yolk. Bake at 180°C/375°F/Gas 5 for 40 minutes.

For the sauce, heat the butter in a heavy pan. Add the flour and cook for 3 minutes stirring continuously. Add the stock to the roux a bit at a time. Whisking continuously reduce the heat and simmer for 30 minutes stirring and skimming every 10 minutes. Add the cream and simmer over a low heat for 10 minutes. Season and pass through a conical sieve into a clean saucepan. Over a low heat, whisk in the butter a little at a time. Remove from the heat, add the sherry and serve with the pheasant.

CDW

Pheasant with Lemon and Capers

I first made this dish at a Red Cross demonstration in Dumfries for Eileen Duncombe. I was somewhat alarmed when I discovered they were going to raffle the food as it was an untried dish. So busy am I these days that I have to invent recipes every time I'm near a stove. However, I'm happy to say this was a success – new pheasant recipes are always welcome.

1 pheasant, cut in strips
zest and juice of 4 lemons
115g/4oz plain flour
salt and freshly ground pepper
4 tbsp oil
1 tbsp capers, roughly chopped
8 tbsp brown sugar
300ml/½ pint game or chicken stock

Marinade the pheasant strips overnight in the lemon juice. Remove meat, reserving the juice, pat dry with kitchen paper and coat with seasoned flour. Brown the strips in the oil in a heavy pan, then add capers, lemon zest and brown sugar, and cook for 2–3 minutes. Heat the stock and lemon juice together and serve as a sauce.

CDW

Duntreath Roast Grouse

This is a perfect way of cooking the slightly older birds you buy later in the season. Some people actually prefer grouse cooked this way, whatever the age.

1 grouse per person
apples
butter
salt and freshly ground pepper
streaky bacon rashers

Place a piece of apple and a knob of butter inside each bird. Season inside and out with salt and pepper and wrap well in streaky bacon. Stand in 1cm/1/2in of water in a roasting tin and cover with a lid of foil. Roast in a preheated oven at 150°C/300°F/Gas 2 for 45 minutes.

Remove the foil lid and pour the liquid from the tin. Unwrap the bacon. Zap up the oven temperature to hot, 230°C/450°F/Gas 8, and roast for 10 minutes more to brown the birds.

CDW

Grouse Pie

If you have a good game butcher he will sell you old grouse quite cheaply as everyone wants the young birds for roasting. This is a flavoursome robust country pie and the gravy is enriched by the addition of steak. This was a custom which grew in the Georgian age with the greater availability of beef, thanks to the Agricultural Revolution.

a brace of grouse
450g/1lb beef, rump or topside
55g/2oz diced bacon
2 eggs, hardboiled
salt and freshly ground pepper
pinch of mace
pinch of nutmeg
600ml/1 pint game stock
1 tbsp sherry
550g/1¼ lb puff pastry
beaten egg, to glaze

Divide each grouse into four leg and four breast pieces, cut the steak into 2.5cm/1in cubes. Arrange in a 1.75ml/3 pint pie dish and top with the bacon and the hardboiled eggs. Pour on enough stock to cover. Put a lid on the dish, or cover with foil and cook in a preheated oven at 160°C/325°F/Gas 3 for 1½ hours. Remove from oven and turn heat up to 220°C/425°F/Gas 7. Allow dish to cool slightly, add sherry, cover with a lid of the puff pastry and bake for a further 30 minutes. Serve with creamed potatoes and green vegetables.

CDW

Medallions of Venison
with Bramble Jelly or Blackberries

Try to get some well-hung venison if you like the gamey taste.

2–3 medallions of venison per person
unsmoked streaky bacon, cut into strips
seasoned flour
the best bramble jelly you can find *or* blackberries, red wine and sugar
really good meat stock
sour cream or crème fraîche
salt and freshly ground pepper

Fry enough bacon very gently to extract enough fat to fry the medallions. Remove the bacon pieces (you can sprinkle them on a salad). Put enough well-seasoned flour into a plastic bag and toss the pieces of venison in it; remove and lay on some greaseproof paper. Heat the bacon fat and fry the meat on a medium heat for 5–7 minutes, turning frequently. Put them in a warmed dish with a teaspoon of bramble jelly on each medallion and keep warm while you make the sauce.

If you are using blackberries instead of jelly, cook them lightly in a little red wine with sugar to taste. Spoon over the medallions as for the jelly.

Depending on how much you are cooking, add enough of the meat stock to the pan you fried the meat in. Boil briskly, stirring all the juices together. When it starts to look syrupy, mix in enough sour cream or crème fraîche to make a rich sauce. Adjust the seasoning. Pour over the venison. Serve with tiny Brussels sprouts and egg noodles with chestnuts if you have some handy. Apple sauce can also be added as a side dish.

JP

Pigeon Breast with Honey and Ginger

The late Archie Coates was probably the world's most famous pigeon shot, and his wife Prue, author of several excellent game cookbooks, may well have cooked more pigeons than anyone else. I am indebted to her for this delicious recipe. It is equally good hot or cold. The quantities given for the sauce will make more than needed, so you can have great fun finding other uses for it.

8 pigeon breasts
55g/2oz butter
juice of ½ lemon
salt and freshly ground pepper

FOR THE SAUCE:
85g/3oz sugar
150ml/¼ pint water
115g/4oz stem ginger
2 tbsp runny honey

For the sauce, dissolve the sugar in the water and boil for 4 minutes without stirring. In a blender pulverise the ginger, add the honey and process, gradually pouring in the sugar syrup. Blend till smooth. This can be done in advance and kept in the fridge.

Heat the butter in a frying pan till foaming and cook the pigeon breasts for 3 minutes each side. Add 4 tbsp of the ginger sauce and cook for a minute more. Remove the pigeon breasts, slice them lengthways and fan out on warmed plates. Add the lemon juice to the pan and cook until the sauce is thick and syrupy. Season to taste. Pour the sauce over the pigeon breasts and serve hot. If serving cold, add thinly sliced fennel dressed with oil and lemon juice.

CDW

Quail

Quail are dear little mouthfuls, but as they are no longer wild they have very little flavour. However, they are very tender and good to eat when tarted up in various guises.

These were excellent.

4 quail
55g/2oz unsalted butter
2 cloves of garlic, crushed
1 tbsp honey
juice of 1 lemon
salt and freshly ground
black pepper

Melt the butter in a little frying pan, add the garlic and sauté gently until softened but not browned. Add the honey and lemon juice. Stir until mixed, then season generously with salt and black pepper.

Place the quail in a small roasting tin and pour the contents of the pan over them. Brush the insides of the birds with some of the juices. Roast in a preheated oven at 230°C/450°F/Gas 8 for 10 minutes. Remove from the oven, baste with the juices and finish off under the grill until they are burnished and browned. Serve with a good salad.

JP

Salmi of Game

This nice old-fashioned dish should ideally be made with half-roasted gamebirds starting from scratch, but I find it a useful way to use up the remains of half-eaten birds. If you go to a dinner party during the game season you often see untutored people merely toying with their birds, leaving a wealth of good meat on the carcass. In such cases I beg the left-overs from mine host and render them into the desired Salmi. Here I give you the authentic method.

any form of game bird roasted very rare, to produce about 450g/1lb meat
4 shallots, finely chopped, and 1 whole shallot
a bouquet garni including a blade of mace
black peppercorns
thinly pared rind of 1 orange
salt and freshly ground pepper
55g/2oz butter
1 heaped tbsp plain flour
150ml/¼ pint red or white wine
115g/4oz mushrooms, sliced and sautéed in butter
lemon juice
bread for croûtons

Carve the meat off the bones into slices as neatly as possible. Reserve. Remove any skin or fat, bash the carcasses and place together in a saucepan. Leave in the hearts and livers, but remove the rather bitter spongy substance from the insides. Cover with water or stock. Add a whole shallot, the bouquet garni, a few peppercorns and the orange rind. Bring to the boil and simmer for about an hour. Strain, return to the saucepan and reduce to 450ml/¾ pint of stock. Season.

In another saucepan, large enough to receive all the ingredients, melt the butter and fry the chopped shallots until soft and yellow. Add the flour and cook for a couple of minutes, then pour in the stock little by little, stirring away to make a sauce. Let it simmer for half an hour or more until quite thick. Add the wine and the mushrooms. Simmer for 5 minutes.

Turn the heat very low. Place the slices of meat in the sauce to heat through for 10 minutes; on no account let them boil which would ruin them. Check seasoning and add a touch of lemon juice to taste. Have ready some good white bread fried crisp in butter. Arrange the Salmi in the centre of a warmed dish and surround with snippets of the bread. Serve with a salad.

JP

Elizabethan Rabbit

A rabbit warren was part of the live larder of an Elizabethan home. Rabbits were still hard to rear and so were regarded as luxury food. It has been said that the Middle Ages ended at the Battle of Bosworth in 1485, but the Elizabethans were still close enough in culinary terms to enjoy the use of fruit in meat dishes, a practice which I believe had come back from the Crusades.

1 rabbit, jointed
plain flour for dusting
55g/2oz lard or dripping
3 Jerusalem artichokes, sliced
2 onions, finely chopped
2 carrots, diced
55g/2oz mushrooms, sliced
300ml/½ pint red wine
a faggot of herbs
2 apples, peeled and chopped
115g/4oz grapes, halved and deseeded
55g/2oz raisins
grated rind and juice of ½ orange
150ml/¼ pint stock
salt and freshly ground pepper

Flour the rabbit joints and brown them well in lard or dripping in a casserole. Remove. Fry the artichokes, onions, carrots and mushrooms in the casserole for a few minutes. Pour over the wine and reduce slightly. Return the rabbit pieces and add all the other ingredients. Cook in a preheated oven at 180°C/350°F/Gas 4 for 2 hours.

A variation on this dish, which I like very much, is to stop the cooking at 1½ hours, transfer to a pie dish, add hard-boiled eggs and globe artichoke hearts, cover with a pastry lid and bake to serve as a pie.

CDW

Rabbit with Mustard

In their brilliant book *The Complete Mustard*, Robin Weir and Ros Mann give this traditional recipe. I love it and serve it often. My mother was Australian so I find it impossible to be sentimental about rabbit. Myxomatosis and bad cooking drove it from our daily diet with displays of the same panic that we are now exercising over beef. Wild rabbit should be soaked in milk overnight if the taste is too strong for you.

1 rabbit, quartered
1 tbsp olive oil
115g/4oz unsalted butter
salt and freshly ground pepper
4–6 tbsp Dijon mustard
2 shallots, finely chopped
225g/8oz button mushrooms, sliced
4 tbsp brandy
300ml/½ pint double cream
a bunch of parsley, finely chopped

Heat the oil and butter in a large pan and lightly brown the rabbit joints. Remove them from the pan, season with salt and pepper, and smear all over with mustard.

Sauté the shallots for 5 minutes, then stir in the mushrooms. Return the rabbit pieces to the pan, pour over the brandy and ignite. When the flames have burnt out, stir in the cream and bring to boiling point. Cover and simmer for 30 minutes until the sauce is thick and the meat tender.

Adjust the seasoning and sprinkle over the parsley. Serve hot.

CDW

Rabbit Isabel

My friend Isabel produced this recipe for me from the Borders. I cooked it at the Scone Palace Game Fair, which is a great event of the Scottish year and was originally set up by my friend Henry Crichton-Stuart. When I demonstrated it they presented me with two whole rabbits, which I cut up on stage. It is a fine recipe for using all the rabbit, is delicious and economical.

1 young rabbit per person, fillets and leg meat removed
25g/1oz plain flour
salt and freshly ground pepper
¼ tsp dry mustard
¼ tsp cayenne pepper
1 egg white
1 slice good bacon per two rabbit fillets
sorrel or sage leaves
115g/4oz butter
1 onion, finely chopped
glass of white wine

Make seasoned flour with salt, pepper, dry mustard and cayenne pepper. In a food processor finely mince the leg meat, add the egg white and seasoning and blend to a paste. Flatten the fillets and flour lightly. Lay a piece of bacon cut to fit on one fillet, spread a layer of the mousseline of rabbit and egg white onto the bacon and lay your sorrel or sage leaves on top of this. Place the other rabbit fillet on top to make a parcel.

In a heavy-lidded frying pan melt the butter and gently fry the onion, add the rabbit parcel and brown, turning carefully. Season, pour on white wine, cover and cook gently for 10 minutes turning the parcel halfway through. Check that the rabbit is tender, and serve with garlic-puréed potatoes and a green vegetable.

CDW

Illustrated overleaf

SIDE DISHES, SALADS AND SAUCES

Whatever the weather the show must go on

To me the making or breaking of any menu rests with the accompaniments to the main course. It is all very well to have a splendid central dish but so often one sees the cook's concentration wavering when it comes to the vegetables. I am very lucky to have so many friends who grow their own vegetables and give me their surplus, but I have to admit it is very hard to buy decent vegetables. I don't know what happens to our own home-grown vegetables, we are told the growers are in thrall to the supermarkets but if you check the shelves they are full of foreign imports. Supermarket vegetables are irradiated, chilled out of existence and tasteless, so the only thing to do is to use them as a base and add other flavours to them.

When designing your menu, remember that in a piece of jewellery every minor stone plays its part. There is nothing worse than bowls of unadorned vegetables untouched by butter or oil or a sprinkling of parsley or whatever. Restaurants have real problems with this and either serve you a demi-lune salad dish full of uninteresting flaccid sad little objects or increasingly no vegetables at all save a token infant by way of garnish.

Buy the best vegetables you can, if they don't have much taste do something to them until they do and mound your serving bowls high to give a feeling of abundance – if you do have any leftovers, you could always try making some soup with them.

Jennifer is adamant that, with the exception of potatoes and a few root crops, vegetables should never touch water – or at most only the water that adheres after they have been rinsed and well shaken. Nothing, she declares firmly, beats a young broad bean. We both love bitter greens, especially chicory, but beg to differ on the carrot. It is my one aversion in the food world and that is for psychological reasons!

If you can grow your own do, or schmooze a friend who does. If this isn't possible, go to a good greengrocer or farm shop. Don't be suckered by the prettiness myth. In the vegetable, true beauty is only skin deep.

Frittata with Tomatoes, Onions and Basil

If you have a barbecue going you can make this 'omelette' outside. I ate it first in Tuscany where it can have many variations – it is an excellent way of using up any left-over vegetables, pasta, ham and cheese and it is particularly good cold. Very different to the rapid cooking of a French omelette, this Italian version is cooked over a low heat, very gently, so is very easy to cook when doing other tasks.

6 medium onions, thinly sliced
6 tbsp olive oil
225g/8oz plum tomatoes
salt and freshly ground pepper
6 eggs (size 1 or 2)
2 tbsp freshly grated Parmesan
a handful of fresh basil
55g/2oz butter

Sweat the onions in the oil until quite soft and just browning. Skin and chop the tomatoes (you can also use tinned ones drained) and add to the onions with a little salt to taste. Cook for 10 minutes, stirring occasionally. Press the vegetables to the side of the pan and remove to a bowl with a slotted spoon. Leave to cool.

Beat the eggs until well mixed but not frothy. Add the vegetables, cheese, a good quantity of ground black pepper and more salt to your liking. Tear up the basil leaves, add and stir everything together. Melt the butter in a 30cm/12in non-stick frying pan until it is just foaming. Pour in the egg mixture, lower the heat and cook for about 15 minutes until the eggs are set but the top is still a bit runny. Then you can put the pan under the grill for half a minute.

Loosen the frittata with a pliable spatula and slide on to a suitable dish. Cut into wedges when cooled. It can be eaten warm with a salad or cold on a hunk of bread, as Italian schoolchildren and workmen do for their lunch.

JP

Illustrated overleaf

Parsnips Roasted with Mace and Brandy

This is from Michelle Beridale Johnson's good little British Museum cookbook.
It is an unusual way of serving parsnips, which works very well.

6 parsnips, trimmed but not peeled
25g/1oz butter
½ wineglass of brandy
1 tsp ground mace

Boil the parsnips for 15 minutes. Cool slightly, then peel and slice. Heat the butter, brandy and mace in a pan, put in the parsnips and heat through. Reduce to a glaze and serve hot.

CDW

Bubble and Squeak

I once lived with a man who could be stopped in midsentence of even the most savage row if I started making this dish. You may imagine I am something of an expert at it.

There are three things to remember:

1. There is no substitute for lard or beef dripping – if you object, eat something else.

2. You need a really heavy frying pan.

3. The potatoes must be cold before you start.

450g/1lb cold potatoes
55g/2oz dripping or lard
1 onion, finely chopped
225g/8oz cooked cabbage or sprouts, chopped
salt and freshly ground pepper

Finely chop the potatoes and crush slightly. In a frying pan melt half of the fat and lightly fry the onion. Mix in the potato and greens and season well with salt and pepper. Add more dripping or lard. Press the bubble into the hot fat and fry over a moderate heat until browned underneath – about 15 minutes. Turn the bubble over, add the last of the dripping or lard and fry until the other side is browned.

CDW

Illustrated overleaf

Hot Curried Cabbage

During the winter when there is a poor variety of fresh vegetables and a lot of cabbage, this makes an interesting way of dealing with that estimable, if somewhat dull, vegetable.

½ a large cabbage, shredded
1 bayleaf
2 cloves of garlic
250ml/8fl oz stock
1 onion
2 cloves
flour
salt and freshly ground pepper
1 tbsp curry powder
3 tbsp butter
120ml/4fl oz cream
55g/2oz dried breadcrumbs

Put the cabbage in a large pan, add the stock, bayleaf and garlic. Stick the cloves into the onion and add to the cabbage. Cook over a medium heat for 10 minutes. Drain the cabbage and discard the bayleaf and the onion. Put the cabbage into a greased casserole dish. Mix together salt, pepper, curry powder and half the butter, add cream and stir until smooth. Pour over the cabbage. Sprinkle on breadcrumbs, dot with remaining butter and bake at 180°C/350°F/Gas 4 for 20 minutes.

CDW

Peas with Lettuce

Test the peas occasionally for taste and tenderness. I often add chopped spring onions to this receipt, but this is optional.

85g/3oz of butter
1.2litre/2pints fresh shelled peas
2 lettuce hearts, tied up with string
1 bouquet garni
1½ tsp salt
2 tsp sugar
3 tbsp water
150ml/¼ pint double cream

Melt the butter in a saucepan, add peas, lettuce hearts, bouquet garni, salt, sugar and water. Simmer with the lid on for 40 minutes. Remove lettuce and strain peas, reserving the liquid. The amount of liquid should be very little but reduce it to about two tablespoonfuls, whisk in the cream and pour over peas. Cut lettuce hearts into quarters and place on the peas.

JP

Baked Beetroot with Sour Cream and Mint

I learnt this recipe years ago from one of my greatest friends, Nandy Routh, wife of Jonathan (the original Candid Camera man). Alas she was killed in a motor accident but this splendid vegetable dish, originally Persian I think, always reminds me of her.

raw beetroots
olive oil
salt and freshly ground pepper
sour cream
finely chopped fresh mint or
good dried mint

I find the long triangular beetroots are best for this dish but it really doesn't matter. Place as many of the beets as you deem necessary in a roasting tin or baking tray. Caress them with olive oil and season with salt and pepper. Bake in a preheated oven at 200°C/400°F/Gas 6 for about 1 hour or until tender to the pierce of a sharp knife or skewer. Serve, split open with a good dollop of sour cream and a generous sprinkling of chopped mint.

JP

Gratin of Beetroot

I love beetroot, its wonderful medieval colour cheering us in the grey months, its texture and sweetness, and the way it lends itself so well to pickles and chutneys. This recipe comes from the late great Jane Grigson's *Vegetable Book*, a volume I open every time I cook for company.

55g/2oz butter
3 tbsp grated mature Cheddar
2 tbsp Parmesan
6 beetroot, boiled, skinned and cubed
salt and freshly ground pepper
6 anchovy fillets
300ml/½ pint double cream
breadcrumbs

Butter a gratin dish and sprinkle a third of the cheese over it. Put in half the beetroot. Season well and spread over it another third of cheese, lay on the anchovy fillets, repeat with the rest of the beetroot and the cheese, packing in well. Pour over enough cream to come to the top of the beetroot. Scatter with a few breadcrumbs and dot with bits of butter. Bake for about 15 minutes in a fairly hot oven 200°C/400°F/Gas 6 until bubbling and golden brown.

CDW

Jerusalem Artichokes with Fine Herbs

This is a delicious vegetable dish, particularly good with poultry or even game. I love it, although its disadvantage is that it tends to create quite a lot of wind, but never mind.

450g/1lb artichokes, peeled and rinsed
salt and freshly ground pepper
2 shallots, finely chopped
1 clove of garlic, finely chopped
25g/1oz butter
1 tbsp flour
300ml/½ pint milk
pinch of grated nutmeg
½ tbsp chopped chives
1 tbsp chopped parsley

Cut the artichokes into evenly sized pieces, cover with water in a saucepan, add a teaspoon of salt, bring to the boil and simmer for about 30 minutes. Check to see if they are cooked, then strain. Meanwhile melt the butter in a saucepan, cook the shallots and garlic gently until they are soft but not coloured. Blend in the flour with a wooden spoon, add the milk gradually, stirring constantly, then add the grated nutmeg. When the sauce has thickened to a nice consistency add a ¼ teaspoon of pepper, chives and most of the parsley, and stir into the artichokes. Sprinkle remaining parsley over the whole mixture.

JP

French Beans with Bacon and Tomato

A variation on the ever-popular French bean. This can be used as a side dish or even as a first course, or as an addition to pasta.

150g/6oz diced bacon
300ml/½ pint stock
750g/1½lb French beans
5 medium tomatoes, peeled, de-seeded and coarsely chopped
salt and fresh ground black pepper
1 tbsp chopped parsley

Put the bacon and stock into a pan, bring to the boil and simmer bacon for 20 minutes, then add the beans, tomatoes and black pepper. Taste for salt as it should not be necessary to add any unless the bacon is very mild. Bring back to the boil and simmer over a low heat until the beans are cooked. Strain the beans, bacon and tomatoes into a serving dish. The beans may lose a bit of colour but their flavour will be enhanced. Sprinkle with parsley and serve.

JP

Boston Baked Beans

Long before the Plymouth Rock landed on the Pilgrim fathers (or was it the other way round?), the staple diet of the English was the baked bean. That stalwart of middle America, *The Joy of Cooking*, in a burst of what might be anti-British sentiment, says that baked beans are as common in Sweden as they are in the USA. This came as something of a surprise to my Swedish friends. Indeed, Sophie Dow, a well-known Swedish food writer, commented that '*Bruna-bonor-och flask*' (brown beans with pork) was commonly used as a threat to control badly behaved children. Like it or not America, the baked bean is another legacy from us British.

There is an eighteenth-century rhyme about the diet of the English working man that runs: 'If you cannot give him bacon – you need not give him beans.' Before the potato inveigled its way into our hearts we all ate beans. They were the favourite food of Elizabeth I, who insisted on the addition of winter savoury to the dish to kill the flatulent effects.

350g/12oz dried navy or haricot beans
a 115g/4oz piece of salt pork
2–3 tbsp tomato ketchup
1 tsp salt
½ tsp vinegar
1 onion, chopped
2 tbsp blackstrap molasses
1 tbsp English mustard powder
250ml/8fl oz beer

Soak the beans overnight in water. Drain and cover with fresh water. Bring to the boil and simmer gently for 1½ hours or until tender. Drain the beans (reserve the water) and place in a greased ovenproof dish. Add all the other ingredients. Cover and bake in a preheated oven at 130°C/250°F/Gas ½ for 7–9 hours. Add the reserved bean water if they appear to be drying out. Cook uncovered for the last hour.

CDW

Spinach and Rice

A great comfort, and so good for you too.

2 tbsp virgin olive oil
4 shallots, finely chopped
1 large clove of garlic
150g/6oz long grain rice, cooked
150g/6oz spinach, cooked, drained and liquidised
1 tbsp mint, finely chopped
½ tsp cinnamon
salt and freshly ground pepper

Heat the olive oil in a frying pan, add the shallots and garlic and cook for a few minutes to soften, don't brown or burn. Add rice to frying pan, stir and coat with the oil. Add spinach, mint, cinnamon, salt and pepper and stir. Cook until the contents of the pan are heated through.

JP

Sugar Browned Potatoes

This is a different way of serving new potatoes and is particularly good with the tasteless new potatoes you buy out of season or you know where! Do not, for instance, waste Jersey royals on this recipe. It is also a good way for re-heating cooked left-over new potatoes.

900g/2lb new potatoes
55g/2oz butter
2 tbsp sugar

Scrape the potatoes and cook until tender. Do not under or over-cook, either is a crime.

In a heavy pan melt the butter, add the sugar and cook over a low heat until the sugar begins to caramelise. Add the potatoes and make sure they become well coated in the caramel. Continue this process until the caramel is a good rich brown. Serve at once.

CDW

Pete's Pommy Pommes

This comes from a magnificent Australian friend, Pete Smith, and my nickname for them is Pommy Pommes. Pete served them at a dinner party with roast lamb, but I have used them with game where they are perfect and easier than proper game chips. Not enough is made of potatoes and I think everyone would love this crunchy, succulent method.

450g/1lb waxy potatoes, peeled
olive oil
150ml/¼ pint vegetable or chicken stock
salt and freshly ground pepper
herbs of your choice (parsley, thyme, tarragon, etc.)
4 cloves of garlic, finely chopped

Slice the potatoes very finely on a mandolin, or with a good, sharp knife or a processor. Steep in cold water for 30 minutes, drain and pat dry. There should only be about 5 layers of potatoes, so choose your roasting pan accordingly. Drizzle some olive oil over the base of the pan. Put a layer of overlapping potato slices on the base, season with salt and freshly ground pepper, a sprinkling of herbs and garlic, a drizzle of olive oil and moisten with a little stock. Continue in this manner until everything is used up. Place in a pre-heated oven at 190°C/375°F/Gas 5 until softish when pierced, then increase the heat to 230°C/450°F/Gas 8 until very brown and crisp. Serve with what you will.

JP

Spaghetti Estivi Freddi
(Summer Spaghetti – Cold)

Originally from the Isle of Ischia, this is a Roman spaghetti salad.

675g/1½lb spaghetti
3 plump cloves of garlic,
crushed
5 tbsp best olive oil
a handful of fresh mint leaves
(spearmint is best),
finely chopped
5 tbsp fresh orange juice
12 black olives
6 anchovy fillets
115g/4oz button mushrooms,
preserved in oil
salt

Cook the garlic gently in the oil until golden. Add the mint and take off the heat. Pour in the orange juice. Chop the olives and anchovies roughly and stir into the pan, then add the mushrooms. Season with salt and mix all together.

Cook the spaghetti in lots of boiling water, keeping them slightly more *al dente* than usual. Drain and pour on to a large platter. Mix in the sauce and spread out to cool. When cool, transfer to a nice rustic bowl to serve.

JP

Tabboule Salad

You can eat Tabboule in your fingers if you are an experienced Middle-Eastern eater.

85g/3oz burghul wheat
4 spring onions, finely chopped
4 heaped tbsp chopped parsley
3 tbsp chopped fresh mint
salt and freshly ground pepper
4 tbsp olive oil
juice of 1 small lemon
2 tomatoes, peeled and chopped

Put the burghul in a sieve and rinse well, then leave to soak in cold water to cover for 30 minutes. Drain well and squeeze dry. Put the burghul in a bowl and add the spring onions, squeezing them with the burghul to release the juices. Add the parsley, mint, salt and pepper. Add the olive oil and lemon juice and toss together thoroughly. Leave in a cool place for a short while to allow the flavours to mingle. Add the chopped tomatoes just before serving. I sometimes add a little diced cucumber, but this too should be added just before serving as the liquid given off by the cucumber can spoil the texture of the salad.

JP

Illustrated overleaf

Ham and Celeriac Salad

A lovely comforting salad for a picnic, this is much loved by border poachers and reivers. This is as made by my friend Isabel Rutherford.

450g/1lb celeriac
1 fresh sharp English apple
(even a Bramley's Seedling)
juice of 1 lemon
salt and freshly ground pepper
2 tbsp Taylors Newport Pagnal
mustard, or other strong
English mustard
300ml/½ pint mayonnaise
1 celery heart, finely diced
225g/8oz good ham, thickly
sliced from the bone

Coarsely grate the celeriac and apple into lemon juice, tossing frequently to prevent discoloration. Season, then add the mustard, mayonnaise, diced celery and ham. Mix well.

CDW

Tomato Tart

A tomato tart looks wonderful with its dramatic colours. This is really a left-over salad Niçoise that I put into a pie crust one day. If you use a piece of fresh tuna it is even better and more sophisticated.

FOR THE SHORTCRUST PASTRY:
115g/4oz plain flour
25g/1oz butter
25g/1oz lard
1 tbsp freshly grated Parmesan cheese (optional)
salt
cold water

FOR THE FILLING:
450g/1lb tomatoes
2 tbsp olive oil
1 clove of garlic, finely chopped
1 medium onion, finely chopped
1 tsp oregano
salt and freshly ground pepper
6 anchovy fillets, chopped or small can of tuna or 115g/4oz piece of fresh tuna
25g/1oz strong Cheddar, grated
2 large eggs
150ml/¼ pint single cream
25g/1oz stoned black olives, chopped

Sift the flour and salt together and rub in the butter and lard until the mixture resembles breadcrumbs. Add the cheese and bind with a little cold water. Chill for 30 minutes and then roll out to line a 20cm/8in flan dish. Chill again for 30 minutes. Cover with foil and baking beans and bake blind in a preheated oven at 200°C/400°F/Gas 6 for 10 minutes. Remove foil and baking beans and cook for a further 5 minutes.

Peel the tomatoes, deseed, slice, strain and save the juice. In a small pan heat the oil over a low heat and sauté the onion until soft, add the garlic and oregano and cook for 1 minute. Add the tomato juice, season and cook till the juice is almost absorbed. Put this in the pastry case and cover with fish. If you are using fresh tuna cook it in a pan with a little more oil for about 2 minutes turning as necessary, then flake it. Cover with tomatoes and grated cheese. Whisk the eggs with the cream and pour over the tomatoes, scattering the olives on top. Bake in a preheated oven at 200°C/400°F/Gas 6 for 15–20 minutes. Serve hot or cold with a green salad, or a salad of green beans, or deep fried French beans which you have dipped in batter.

CDW

Illustrated overleaf

Stuffed Artichokes

We don't make enough of artichokes in this country. I was once paid to go and teach etiquette to Yuppies and one of the items on the agenda was the correct way to eat artichokes! Come back Queen Victoria! Eat them as you feel inspired and use your fingers.

6 large globe artichokes
85g/3oz fresh breadcrumbs
1 onion, finely chopped
115g/4oz Parmesan, coarsely grated
4 tbsp chopped parsley
2 cloves of garlic, finely chopped
2 tomatoes, peeled, deseeded and chopped
1 tbsp capers, cut in half
55g/2oz black olives, stoned and chopped
salt and freshly ground pepper
olive oil
150ml/¼ pint white wine

Remove the large outside leaves from the artichokes. Cut 2.5cm/1in off the top of the remaining leaves and scoop out the choke from the centre of each artichoke.

Make a stuffing by mixing together the remaining ingredients, except the oil and wine, and fill the centre of the artichokes. Cover the bottom of a heavy casserole, large enough to hold the artichokes comfortably, with olive oil. Heat until it is warm, then add the artichokes. Pour over the white wine, cover and simmer gently for about 1 hour.

CDW

Broccoli with Corn and Chorizo Sauce

Like the former American President George Bush I am not that fond of broccoli, although I love purple sprouting broccoli. However it is sometimes the only green vegetable around and this is a good way of enlivening it. If you want to make it more substantial, you can add more *chorizo* sausage and have it as a supper dish.

750g /1½lb broccoli
115g/4 oz butter
4 shallots, chopped
450g/1lb corn kernels
2 tbsp water
pinch of nutmeg
115g/4oz *chorizo* sausage, chopped
salt and freshly ground pepper

Separate the broccoli into florets. Melt 55g/2oz butter in a pan, add the broccoli and stir to coat with butter. Add water to cover and cook for about 10 minutes or until just tender, but still crunchy. In a pan melt the remaining butter, add shallots and corn and cook until the shallots are soft. In a food processor blend this mixture adding a little water. Return to the pan, add the nutmeg, sausage and seasonings, and gently heat through. Thin if too thick and pour over the broccoli.

CDW

Proper Bread Sauce

This much beloved sauce can be a terrible disappointment when served in hotels and restaurants and I'm afraid in many people's houses. The French have never seen the point of it, though I have made a few converts. It couldn't be simpler, the all important point being the flavouring of the milk. There is never enough sauce so make a lot. It is delicious served cold with the remains of a bird.

1 onion
10 cloves or more, to taste
600ml/1 pint full cream milk
25g/1oz butter
1 bayleaf
about 12–16 tbsp fresh white breadcrumbs, made from day-old good bread
300ml/½ pint double cream
salt and freshly ground pepper
freshly grated nutmeg

Peel the onion and stud it with the cloves. Place in a saucepan with the milk, butter and bayleaf. Bring to the boil and simmer on a low heat for 2 minutes. Remove from the heat, cover and let it steep all day to absorb the flavours. When nearly ready to serve, heat again, then add the breadcrumbs a few tablespoons at a time until you get the right consistency, remembering that they will swell. (I make the breadcrumbs in a food processor which is fast and easy.) Add the cream, season well with salt and pepper and finally with a good scraping of nutmeg. Remove the onion and bayleaf, transfer to a well-warmed sauce-boat and serve with whatever you had in mind.

JP

Skordalia

Skordalia is a Greek version of aioli mayonnaise but made without eggs. It goes well with fish, fowl or vegetables and is most useful as a picnic sauce instead of mayonnaise, which goes lethal if left in the sun and produces salmonella.

3 fat cloves of garlic
a 5cm/2in thick slice of stale white bread, decrusted
85–115g/3–4oz blanched almonds, grated
125ml/4floz olive oil
salt
wine vinegar

Crush the garlic well in a mortar. Soak the bread in water, then squeeze out the surplus. Add to the garlic in the mortar and pound away, gradually mixing in the grated almonds until you have a nice homogenous paste. Start adding the oil drop by drop as for mayonnaise and finishing with a steady stream. Finally, season with salt and vinegar to your taste.

JP

PUDDINGS, CAKES AND PASTRIES

Picnicking in Cambridge

Many a bad meal has been saved by a good pudding. However poor the rest of the meal, if your guests finish with an excellent dessert, they will go away with a better memory of it. I know a restaurant which seems to work on that principle, and which has flourished for years. Jennifer does not really like puddings; she accepts that they are a necessity of life and that she must make them for her friends, but she is really happier finishing a meal with some cheese. That does not mean that she does not make some very inspired examples, but it is not a passion of hers. I, however, live in Scotland, a country with a very sweet tooth. I sometimes think that my guests spend the meal in suspended animation, waiting for the pudding. One good thing about puddings is that one can usu-ally make them in advance so that time is on your side. On an everyday level one may not always have time to make a pudding, but good, home-grown fruit in summer or some fruit purée from the freezer in winter – or even better, some bottled fruit – always make an easy dessert.

Anyone can learn to make puddings, cakes and pastries. True pâtissières, however, are born, not made: they have iced water in the veins of their hands and are thin and nervous from the strains of perfection. I am not one of their num-ber, but I get real pleasure from baking and I have learnt certain things.

Whilst other cookery has room for error and a freehand style, it is important to measure care-fully in baking … to be thorough in your folding, creaming and measuring … and to line your baking tins carefully and butter them, when directed, as thoroughly as *Last Tango in Paris*. It is also important to remember, for your own self-worth, that even the most experienced bakers have off days, and that fruit inexplicably sinks in fruit cakes. Sweet baking is always done with unsalted butter, and most good bakers use plain flour and add their own quantity of baking pow-der. There are endless theories about flour. I tend to use strong flour for bread, ordinary plain flour for pastry and self-raising flour for cakes. Use caster sugar unless told otherwise, and make sure your scales are accurate.

Eton Mess

This must be one of the easiest puddings to make. Other suitable fruits, such as raspberries, also look luscious.

450g/1lb strawberries
85g/3oz caster sugar
2 tsp Kirsch
6 small meringues
600ml/1 pint double cream, whipped until thick

Crush the strawberries lightly, and sprinkle with the sugar and Kirsch. Leave in the fridge for 2–3 hours. Crush the meringues coarsely and fold into the strawberries with the whipped cream.

JP

Almond and Lemon Flan

A rich offering but usually irresistible. It can be produced as a pudding or for a tea party.

FOR THE FLAN CASE:
150g/5oz plain flour
pinch of salt
85g/3oz butter
25g/1oz ground almonds
2 tsp grated lemon rind
1 egg, beaten
a little water

FOR THE FILLING:
150g/5oz caster sugar
55g/2oz butter, at room temperature
3 eggs
grated rind and juice of 2 lemons
115g/4oz ground almonds
150ml/¼ pint double cream, whipped until thick
1 tsp almond essence
icing sugar for sprinkling

To make the flan case, sift the flour and salt together and rub in the butter until the mixture resembles fine crumbs. Stir in the ground almonds and lemon rind. Bind with the beaten egg, plus 1–2 tsp of water if necessary, to make a firm dough. Chill for half an hour, then roll out to line a 20cm/8in loose-bottomed flan tin. Chill once again for 20 minutes if possible.

Prick the bottom of the flan case with a fork and line with grease-proof paper. Fill with dried baking beans and bake in a preheated oven at 180°C/350°F/Gas 4 for 15 minutes. Remove the beans and greaseproof paper, then return to oven and bake for a further 5 minutes. Remove from the oven, and reduce the heat to 150°F/300°F/Gas 2.

For the filling, beat the sugar, butter, eggs and grated lemon rind together. Add the almonds, almond essence and lemon juice. Fold in the whipped cream and pour into the flan case. Bake for about 40 minutes or until the filling is just set. Allow to cool, then dust the top with icing sugar.

JP

Apple Strudel

You will find this famous national dish in every cake shop and cafe in Austria and Germany, not to mention Soho. Don't be frightened by the filo pastry, it is quite easy to manage as long as you keep it moist. I prefer to use Bramley apples for strudel.

450g/1lb of cooking apples, peeled, cored and cut into thin slices
55g/2oz caster sugar
½ tsp cinnamon
40g/1½oz sultanas
40g/1½oz walnuts, finely chopped
1 tsp grated lemon rind
8 sheets filo pastry
85g/3oz melted butter
2 tbsp white breadcrumbs

In a mixing bowl, combine apples, caster sugar, cinnamon, sultanas, walnuts and lemon rind. Keep the filo pastry covered with a damp cloth to prevent it drying out. Lay a sheet of filo pastry on a damp cloth, brush with melted butter and cover with a thin layer of breadcrumbs. Put another sheet of filo pastry on top and repeat the process. Arrange a 2.5cm/1in thick roll of apple mixture 5cm/2in from the end of the filo pastry nearest to you. Lift up the end of the damp cloth nearest you, the filo pastry will begin to roll over. Firm the filo over the apple mixture and then continue to roll to get a jam roll effect. Repeat with the rest of the filo and apple mixture. Bake in a preheated oven at 220°C/425°F/Gas 7 for 10 minutes, then reduce the heat to 200°C/400°F/Gas 6 and cook for a further 20 minutes, or until the strudel is crisp and brown.

JP

Quercyan Apple Cake

Usually I keep my recipes very simple but this, though somewhat harder than usual, really repays the effort. Most of my stay in Quercy is either unremembered or censored, but the recipe remains.

450g/1lb plain flour
½ tsp baking powder
2 eggs
40g/1½oz butter, creamed

FOR THE FILLING:
1.5kg/3lb apples, peeled and thinly sliced
225g/8oz sugar
120ml/4fl oz rum
85ml/3fl oz orange flower water
thinly pared rind of 1 lemon

TO FINISH:
25g/1oz butter, melted
1 egg, beaten
caster sugar

Macerate the sliced apples with the filling ingredients overnight. Strain the apples, reserving the juice.

Sift the flour and baking powder into a large bowl, put butter and eggs into a well in the centre. Working with the fingertips gradually add 200ml/7fl oz of the liquid from the apples. Work into a smooth and elastic paste with your hand and leave to rest for 2 hours. Roll out as thinly as possible, then transfer to a floured cloth on a large table. Working from the centre, with the palms of your hands, carefully stretch the paste to the thinness of a cigarette paper. Rest it and yourself for 1 hour.

Brush lightly with melted butter and dust with sugar, cover with well drained apples and roll up. Mix the remaining juice into the beaten egg and brush over the top. Bake in a preheated oven at 190°C/390°F/Gas 5 for 50–55 minutes.

CDW

Danish Apple and Prune Cake

This is a recipe from the great Australian cook Greta Anna. I hope you love it as much as I do. I had a Danish great-grandmother but she couldn't cook, so thank you Greta Anna.

FOR THE BATTER:
140g/5oz butter
200g/7oz caster sugar
2 eggs, well beaten
85g/3oz self-raising flour
115g/4oz ground almonds
125ml/4floz milk
1 tsp vanilla essence
1 tbsp boiling water
½ tsp baking powder

FURTHER INGREDIENTS:
8 stoned prunes, chopped
115g/4oz shelled walnuts, finely chopped and mixed with 2 tbsp sugar
2 green apples, cored and sliced
3 tbsp sugar
ground cinnamon
butter

Cream together all the ingredients for the batter in a food processor, running it for 10 seconds. Run a spatula round the bowl and process for 5 seconds more. Pour into a well-buttered 25cm/10in round cake tin.

Place the prunes on the batter. Spoon over the walnut and sugar mixture. Arrange the apple slices on top of the walnuts. Bake in a preheated oven at 190°C/375°F/Gas 5 for 45 minutes.

Sprinkle the surface with the sugar and some cinnamon. Dot with butter and bake for a further 20–25 minutes till a skewer comes out clean. Cool in the tin.

CDW

Claret Jelly

This is a grown-up jelly. It has a wonderful colour and smell and looks great turned from a complicated mould. I once made it before 150 of Edinburgh's finest, and so scared was I that it would not set that I added an extra gelatine leaf. It took me three goes to turn it out, which I finally did to the supportive cheers of the crowd! As always, the better the wine, the better the jelly.

2 sachets powdered gelatine
or 5 leaves of gelatine
1 bottle of claret-type wine
½ wineglass of brandy
1 small jar redcurrant jelly
grated rind and juice of 1
orange
55g/2oz caster sugar

Soften the gelatine in a little cold water. Put all the remaining ingredients in a saucepan, bring to the boil and simmer for 10 minutes. Pour on to the gelatine, stirring well until it is completely dissolved. (If using leaf gelatine, drain it and add to the hot liquid, off the heat.) Allow to cool slightly, then pour into a wetted jelly mould. Chill until set. Turn out to serve (if you can, adds my friend, Isabel Rutherford).

CDW

Gooseberry and Elderflower Parfait

This parfait is rather a treat as gooseberries don't have a very long season, although you can purée them in quantities and freeze. The purée is also useful to serve with mackerel.

225g/8oz gooseberries
6 tbsp water
115g/4oz caster sugar
4 egg yolks
2 tbsp elderflower cordial
150ml/¼ pint double cream, whipped until thick

TO SERVE:
whipped cream flavoured with elderflower cordial

Simmer the gooseberries with 3 tbsp of the water until soft. When tender pureé the gooseberries, and then sieve the purée. Very gently heat the sugar with the remaining water until the sugar has dissolved, then bring to the boil and simmer for 2–3 minutes. Remove from the heat. Place the egg yolks in a large bowl and whisk together. While whisking, gradually pour on the sugar syrup, and continue whisking until the mixture is very thick and cold. Whisk in the elderflower cordial, then fold in the lightly whipped cream and the gooseberry purée. Pour the mixture into a 450g/1lb loaf tin lined with cling film and freeze until solid, preferably overnight if possible.

About 15–20 minutes before serving, turn out on to a serving dish and leave to soften in the fridge. Then cut into slices. Put a blob of elderflower-flavoured whipped cream at the side of each serving.

JP

Illustrated overleaf

Lemon Meringue Roulade

With all the books in our shop, there is one food writer I know will never let me down when it comes to puddings, and that is Claire Macdonald. Since I moved to Scotland, Claire and her husband Godfrey, Lord Macdonald have become great friends. They own Kinloch Lodge Hotel on the Isle of Skye. Somehow the beauty of the 'far Cuillins' is greatly enhanced with a plate of this delicious roulade.

5 egg whites
140g/5oz caster sugar
1 level tsp cornflour
icing sugar
300ml/½ pint double cream
6 level tbsp lemon curd

Line the sides and bottom of a 31 x 22cm/12½ x 8½in swiss roll tin with non-stick baking parchment. Whisk the egg whites until white, frothy and doubled in bulk. Add 1 level tbsp caster sugar and whisk until the egg whites are stiff but not too dry. The mixture should fall in soft peaks. Gradually whisk in half of the remaining caster sugar, then continue to whisk until the meringue is very stiff and shiny. With a large metal spoon fold in the remaining caster sugar and the cornflour.

Spoon the meringue into the tin and level the surface. Bake in a preheated oven at 100°C/220°F/Gas ¼ for 45 minutes, or in a four-door Aga, bottom of bottom right oven for 10 minutes then top left oven for 20 minutes or until set. Cool uncovered for 1 hour.

Turn out the meringue on to a sheet of parchment dusted with icing sugar. Peel away the lining parchment from the base. Whip the cream until lightly thickened. Spread the cream over the meringue, then spread with lemon curd. Roll up the roulade from one of the short ends. Serve immediately, dusted with icing sugar.

CDW

Coffee Meringue

This is one of those delightful puddings which can be whipped up in a moment once you have a batch of meringues at your bidding. You can even use bought ones. As I always have many frozen egg whites waiting to be used up I usually have a tin of meringues at the ready. To make meringues, which couldn't be easier, use 2 tbsp caster sugar to each egg white. Whisk the egg whites until really stiff, whisk in half the sugar until stiff again and then fold in the rest of the sugar. Cover the baking tray with non-stick baking parchment and dollop the meringue mixture in dessertspoon-size blobs over the surface as neatly as possible. Bake in a preheated oven at 115°C/240°F/Gas ¼ for 1½ hours. Leave to cool, then turn on to a rack and store in a large tin.

8 meringues
115g/4oz blanched almonds
1 dessertspoon white sugar
300ml/½ pint double cream
1 tbsp good old Camp coffee
freshly ground coffee

Chop up the almonds and heat with the sugar in a frying pan until brown and caramelised, turning them all the time as they can burn in a moment. Turn out to cool on some greaseproof paper. Break up the meringues into a lovely glass bowl. Whip the cream until it stands in soft peaks, mix in the Camp coffee and spoon over the meringues. Scatter the sugared almonds over the pudding and finally sprinkle some freshly ground coffee over the lot.

Delicious, d'lovely and delectable and mostly made of air.

JP

Plum Kuchen

This German delight is full of cream and plums and is very good with a cup of excellent coffee.

115g/4oz brown flour
pinch of baking powder
85g/3oz butter, softened
25g/1oz ground almonds
85g/3oz brown sugar
1 tbsp cinnamon
750g/1½lb ripe Victoria plums,
cut in half and stoned
2 egg yolks
150ml/¼ pint sour cream

Sift the flour and baking powder into a bowl, rub in the softened butter, add the almonds and 55g/2oz of the brown sugar, mix. Press the mixture firmly into a buttered 20–23cm/8–9in flan tin. Arrange the plums, flesh side down, to cover the mixture closely. Sprinkle with cinnamon and the remaining sugar. Bake in a pre-heated oven at 190°C/375°F/Gas 5 for 20–25 minutes.

In the meantime beat the egg yolks with the sour cream and when the plums have been brought out of the oven pour this mixture over the plums and then bake for a further 40 minutes, at the same temperature.

JP

Devil's Food Cake

Why this is called Devil's Food Cake I cannot imagine, far too good for the devil who gets the best tunes already according to Charles Wesley. Perhaps, in the words of David Garrick, it is because 'Heaven sends us good meat, but the Devil sends cooks'. Anyway it is devilishly good.

115g/4oz butter
115g/4oz best plain chocolate
115g/4oz golden syrup
55g/2oz soft brown sugar
½ tsp bicarbonate of soda
4 tbsp milk
225g/8oz self-raising flour
a small pinch of salt
1 egg

FOR THE VANILLA BUTTER ICING:
115g/4oz unsalted butter
225g/8oz icing sugar
6 drops of pure vanilla
essence (not flavouring)

FOR THE AMERICAN FROSTING:
225g/8oz granulated sugar
4 tbsp water
1 egg white
25g/1oz best plain chocolate

Grease and line 2 sandwich tins that are 20cm/8in across.

In a saucepan melt the butter, chocolate, syrup and sugar, stirring regularly (do not boil). Cool. Dissolve the bicarbonate of soda in 1 tbsp of milk. Sift the flour and the salt into a bowl and make a well in the centre. Beat in the chocolate mixture, the remaining milk and the egg, using a wooden spoon, then mix in the dissolved bicarbonate of soda. Place in the prepared tins, dividing equally. Bake in a preheated oven at 160°C/325°F/Gas 3 for 35 minutes, then turn out of the tins to cool on racks. When cool, sandwich together with vanilla butter icing.

To make vanilla butter icing, whizz all the ingredients in a food processor until soft and creamy, or beat together by hand with a wooden spoon. If you prefer, use coffee essence or rum to taste instead of the vanilla.

For the top of the cake make American frosting: Put the sugar and water into a heavy pan and heat gently until the sugar dissolves. Bring to the boil and continue boiling until the syrup reaches 115°C/240°F. If you don't have a sugar thermometer, drop a drop of the syrup into cold water. If it makes a soft ball it is ready. Whisk the egg white to form soft peaks. Pour the syrup gradually on to it, whisking all the time, until the frosting thickens and has a rough granular feel. Pour the frosting over the cake and smooth in whirls with a wet, warm, stainless-steel knife. Sprinkle with grated chocolate just before the frosting sets.

JP

Adult Chocolate Cake

Here is a cake to satisfy the chocoholics to the fill. I say cake, but it contains no flour and is more like a baked mousse with crispy sides. Whatever it is, it is outrageously rich and therefore highly recommendable.

225g/8oz good plain chocolate (Menier, Terry's etc)
225g/8oz unsalted butter, softened
280g/10oz caster sugar
5 eggs

Grease a cake tin 22.5cm/8¾ in diameter and 4cm/1½in deep (approximately).

Break the chocolate into a bowl large enough to receive all the other ingredients. Set over a saucepan of barely simmering water until melted. Remove from the heat and cool slightly. Cut the butter into little pieces and beat into the chocolate. Add the sugar and blend well, beating thoroughly. In another bowl, beat the eggs until very frothy and foamy, then gently fold into the chocolate mixture; make sure everything is thoroughly combined.

Pour the mixture into the cake tin and place it in another oven tin with enough water to come up 2.5cm/1in of the cake tin's side. Bake in a preheated oven at 180°C/350°F/Gas 4 for 1 hour, then let it cool completely in the tin. When cold remove from the water-filled tin and chill in the refrigerator overnight. Do not attempt to eat it while still warm. When ready to eat, run a palette knife round the edge of the tin and with a good thump turn the cake out. Serve with whipped cream or ice cream. It's a killer.

JP

Hot Chocolate Soufflé

Nobody can resist chocolate soufflé unless they're allergic. If you wish you can make just one large soufflé in which case it would take about 30 minutes to cook.

85g/3oz good quality dark chocolate
1 tbsp brandy or rum
25g/1oz butter
25g/1oz plain flour
150ml/¼ pint milk
70g/2½ oz caster sugar
½ tsp vanilla extract
4 eggs, separated

Break up the chocolate and put in a bowl with the brandy or rum. Put the bowl over a saucepan of gently simmering water and allow to melt slowly.

Melt the butter in a saucepan, add the flour and cook over a low heat for a few minutes, stirring constantly. Warm the milk in another saucepan, melt the caster sugar in it and then blend in to the flour and butter. Continue to cook slowly, stirring constantly, until the mixture thickens. Remove the saucepan from the heat, add the vanilla extract and chocolate mixture and mix well. Add the lightly beaten egg yolks and beat well. Whisk the egg whites fairly stiffly and then fold into the chocolate mixture.

Spoon the mixture into individual buttered ramekin dishes and bake in a preheated oven 190°C/375°F/Gas 5 for about 15 minutes or until the soufflés are well risen. Serve immediately.

JP

Chocolate Tart

Nearly everyone loves chocolate, so use the best you can find to make this terrific tart.

115g/4oz plain chocolate
25g/1oz butter
2 eggs
85g/3oz caster sugar
2 tbsp plain flour
4 tbsp double cream
1 x 20cm/8in flan case, baked blind
whipped cream to decorate

Melt the chocolate with the butter, and leave to cool slightly. Whisk the eggs and sugar together until thick, then fold in the cooled chocolate mixture. Gently mix in the sifted flour and then the double cream. Pour into the pastry case. Bake in a preheated oven at 180°C/350°F/Gas 4 for 30 minutes or until the filling is lightly set. Leave to cool overnight, then decorate with piped whipped cream before serving.

JP

Aquitanian Walnut Torte

One of the most remarkable women ever to be Queen of England was Eleanor of Aquitaine. Born in 1122, she divorced the King of France to marry Henry II, and founded the first home for battered wives at Fontreveault Abbey in France. She started the idea of Romantic love and is believed to have introduced the black walnut to England, so I always think of this as her cake. The recipe, however, I owe once again to Greta Anna.

4 eggs, separated
200g/7oz caster sugar
450g/1lb shelled walnuts, ground to fine crumbs
1 tsp baking powder

FOR THE ICING:
450g/1lb icing sugar, sifted
85g/3oz butter, softened
4 tsp finely ground coffee beans softened with a little boiling water

Beat the egg yolks and sugar lightly together until blended. Whisk the egg whites until stiff. Fold into the yolks and sugar, then gently mix in the walnut crumbs and baking powder. Pour into a buttered 20cm/8in round cake tin. Bake in a preheated oven at 170°C/325°F/Gas 3 for 50–55 minutes (test with a skewer). Cool in the tin.

For the icing, gradually beat the icing sugar into the butter and flavour with the coffee. Apply to the cooled cake.

CDW

Chocolate Whisky Cake

Not much whisky here, but enough to give taste to a lovely cake.

85g/3oz sultanas
4 tbsp whisky
175g/6oz plain chocolate
115g/4oz butter or margarine
3 eggs, separated
115g/4oz light soft brown sugar
55g/2oz self-raising flour
¼ tsp freshly grated nutmeg
70g/2½oz chopped walnuts
grated rind of 1 small orange

FOR THE TOPPING:
55g/2oz unsalted butter, at room temperature
200g/7oz icing sugar, sifted
4 tbsp whisky

Soak the sultanas in the whisky for several hours, preferably overnight. Melt the chocolate and butter very gently in a heatproof bowl set over a pan of barely simmering water, then leave to cool. Beat the egg yolks with the sugar until pale and thick. Fold in the cooled chocolate mixture, sultanas with any remaining whisky, the walnuts and grated orange rind. Add the flour and nutmeg and fold in gently. Whisk the egg whites until stiff and fold into the cake mixture. Spoon into a greased 20cm/8in cake tin. Bake in the centre of a preheated oven at 180°C/350°F/Gas 4 for 1 hour, or until a skewer inserted in the centre of the cake comes out clean. Leave in the tin for 15 minutes, then turn out on to a wire rack and leave to cool.

For the topping, cream the butter and sugar together until smooth. Add the whisky and beat until it has been absorbed. Spread over the top of the cake.

JP

Baklava

A popular dessert of the Eastern Mediterranean and Middle East. It seems to have appeared during the time of the Ottoman Empire, therefore its name is Turkish.

175g/6oz chopped walnuts, or use hazelnuts, almonds, pistachio nuts or a mixture of nuts
85g/3oz sugar
1 level tsp ground cinnamon
225g/8oz filo pastry
85g/3oz unsalted butter, melted

FOR THE SYRUP:
150g/5oz granulated sugar
150ml/¼ pint water
1 tbsp lemon juice
a good pinch of ground cinnamon
1 tbsp rosewater or orange flower water

Mix the chopped walnuts with the sugar and cinnamon. Brush a baking tin (I use a swiss roll tin) with melted butter and line it with four sheets of filo pastry, brushing each sheet with melted butter and cutting the sheets to fit the tray. Spread half the nut mixture over the pastry, then cover with two more sheets, each brushed with melted butter. Spread over the remaining nuts and cover with another four sheets of pastry, not forgetting to brush each with melted butter. Brushing the top sheet with the remaining butter. Mark the top in diamond shapes, using a sharp knife. Bake in a preheated oven at 180°C/350°F/Gas 4 for 30–40 minutes or until golden brown, turning the oven up to 190°C/375°F/Gas 5 for the last 10 minutes if the pastry needs browning.

While the baklava is baking make the syrup. Place the sugar, water and lemon juice in a small saucepan and warm over a low heat to dissolve the sugar. Bring to the boil and boil for 2 minutes. Add the cinnamon and rosewater or orange flower water. Pour the hot syrup over the baklava and leave to cool before cutting into the marked diamonds.

JP

Carrotts' Flapjacks

In the distant days when we were starving schoolgirls, I made two friends who have lasted me my life through to date. One of them, Caroline Driver, nicknamed Carrotts, became an instant favourite because she brought with her the most delicious flapjacks I have ever eaten. It put me off anyone else's for life. More years down the line than either of us would willingly admit to, she has given me the recipe.

MAKES 16

175g/6oz demerara sugar
175g/6oz butter
225g/8oz rolled oats
pinch of salt

Melt the sugar and butter together in a saucepan. Mix in the oats and salt. Pour the mixture into a greased and lined 20 x 30cm/8 x 12in tin, and press firmly down into the tin to flatten evenly.

Bake in the centre of a preheated oven at 180°C/350°F/Gas 4 for 30 minutes. When cooked, cut into 16 fingers and leave to cool in the tin. Store in an airtight container.

CDW

Rigo Jancsi Chocolate Slices

Before the days of unsavoury 'travellers', I wonder how many of us dreamed of running away 'with the raggle taggle gypsies oh'. Rigo Jansci could have been the model for the poem. He was a gypsy fiddler beloved of polite society (and boy, was it polite) in Budapest in the 1920s. Unfortunately it emerged that it was rather more than his music that was adored by the ladies, and a huge scandal ensued. An enterprising confectioner devised these delicious slices to cash in on the act. I owe this recipe and the story to a lady's maid who was there at the time.

3 eggs, separated
3 tbsp caster sugar
25g/1oz dark chocolate, grated
2 tbsp plain flour

FOR THE FILLING:
apricot jam
25g/1oz cocoa powder
55g/2oz sugar
vanilla essence
175ml/6floz double cream, stiffly whipped

FOR THE CHOCOLATE ICING:
175g/6oz dark chocolate
25g/1oz unsalted butter

Cream together the egg yolks and sugar. Whisk the egg whites until very stiff. Add the grated chocolate and flour to the yolk mixture, then fold in the egg whites. Line and grease a 1½lb loaf tin and pour in the chocolate mixture. Bake in a preheated oven at 180°C/350°F/Gas 4 for 15–20 minutes. Turn out and cool on a rack. When cold, slice in half lengthways through the middle.

Spread both halves of cake with jam on the cut sides. For the filling, mix together all the remaining ingredients, and spread evenly over one half on top of the jam. Make the icing by melting the chocolate with the butter. Allow to cool slightly, then spread over the jam on the other half. Put the two strips together so that the icing and filling are together in the middle, with the iced strip on top, and chill slightly before slicing to serve.

CDW

Rhum Babas

This is an outrageously sticky pudding, soaking in rum and covered in syrup – a good heart stopper. It was one of my mother's favourite delicacies and she lived to eighty-eight.

25g/1oz fresh yeast
150ml/¼ pint warm milk
225g/8oz strong flour
pinch of salt
55g/2oz caster sugar
3 eggs, beaten
55g/2oz butter, softened
85g/3oz sultanas
pinch of salt
300ml/½ pint freshly whipped cream, to serve

FOR THE SYRUP:
300ml/½ pint water
225g/8oz sugar
6 tbsp rum

Blend yeast, milk and 55g/2oz of the flour in a bowl and leave to stand in a warm place until frothy. Sift the remaining flour and salt into a large bowl and add the caster sugar. Make a well in the centre and add the frothy yeast mixture and mix with a wooden spoon. Gradually beat in the eggs and softened butter. Beat the mixture well, then cover with a cloth and leave to rise until double in bulk. Punch down the dough and knead in the sultanas. Put the dough into small greased ring moulds, half filling them, and leave to rise again until the dough is level with the top of the mould. Cook in a preheated oven at 200°C/400°F/Gas 6 for 15–20 minutes.

To make the syrup, dissolve the sugar in the water over a gentle heat for a few minutes, then stir in the rum. When the babas are cooked, leave them to cool in the moulds for a few minutes, then turn out and immerse in hot syrup. Remove from the syrup and serve with freshly whipped cream.

JP

Orange Gobbet Cakes

How language changes. A gobbet is an eighteenth-century word for a mouthful, a polite and dainty word, perfect to describe these little cakes.

MAKES 48

115g/4oz unsalted butter, at room temperature
115g/4oz caster sugar
finely grated rind and juice of 1 orange
175g/6oz self-raising flour
1 tsp baking powder
2 eggs, beaten
4 pieces of stem ginger, cut into slivers

Cream the butter with the sugar and orange zest. Sift the flour with the baking powder. Mix the flour and beaten eggs alternately into the creamed mixture. Add enough orange juice to give the mixture a dropping consistency.

Butter the smallest tartlet tins and spoon in the mixture. Put a sliver of ginger on each. Bake in a preheated oven at 190°C/375°F/ Gas 5 for 15 minutes or until done.

CDW

Cockaigne Brownies

I got this receipt years ago when I accompanied the sculptor Fiore de Henriquez on a lecture tour round the USA (top part). These are the classic brownies, much my most favourite cake in America, with its chewy texture and rich chocolate flavour. You could always throw in a handful of fresh dried cannabis to liven up a dull tea party – but beware the cops!

MAKES ABOUT 30

115g/4oz best plain chocolate
115g/4oz butter
4 eggs
½ tsp salt
450g/1lb caster sugar
1 tsp best vanilla essence
115g/4oz plain flour
115g/4oz chopped pecans or walnuts
whipped cream (optional)

In a double-boiler or a bowl over a pan of barely simmering water, melt the chocolate and butter. Cool, then beat until foamy and light in colour.

Beat the eggs, which should be at room temperature, with the salt, then gradually add the sugar and vanilla essence, beating all the time until really creamy.

Combine the cooled chocolate mixture with the eggs and sugar, with a few deft strokes, using a spatula, then fold in the sifted flour followed by the pecans or walnuts. Pour into a greased, 22.5x32.5cm/9x13in tin and bake in a preheated oven at 180°C/350°F/Gas 4 for about 25 minutes, or until the centre is just firm to the touch. Do not overcook.

Cool in the tin, then cut into squares. To store, wrap in foil. You can serve the brownies with whipped cream, or just chew them.

JP

Brandy Snaps

Like pancakes, the first brandy snaps you make are a bit ragged, but don't despair. You will get better and better.

MAKES ABOUT 20

55g/2oz butter
2 tbsp golden syrup
55g/2oz caster sugar
55g/2oz plain flour
1 level tsp ground ginger
150ml/¼ pint double cream
1 dessertspoon brandy

Put the butter, golden syrup and sugar into a saucepan and heat gently until melted. Remove from the heat, and stir in the flour and ginger. Grease 2 or 3 baking sheets thoroughly with butter. Put teaspoonfuls of the mixture on the baking sheets, about 7.5cm/3in apart to allow for spreading. Bake in a preheated oven at 170°C/325°F/Gas 3 for 8–10 minutes or until golden brown. Keep an eye on them to make sure they do not get too brown.

In the meantime grease the handle of a wooden spoon. Remove the baking sheets from the oven and leave the biscuits to cool for 2–3 minutes. Then, one at a time, lift them off with a palette knife and roll and press around the wooden spoon. Hold until the snap is set, then slide it off on to a wire rack. If the biscuits become too stiff to roll, return them to the oven briefly to warm and soften.

Whip the cream and add the brandy. Pipe a dollop of cream into each snap.

JP

Fresh Fruit Tartlets

Fancy is as fancy does, and nothing could be fancier than little fruit tartlets. They are good and messy, but a pleasure to the eye and taste.

MAKES ABOUT 10

115g/4oz shortcrust pastry
55g/2oz dark chocolate, melted
115/4oz cream cheese, at room temperature
1 tbsp double cream
15g/½oz caster sugar
a few drops of vanilla essence
fresh fruit (strawberries, raspberries, sliced peaches etc)
apricot jam or redcurrant jelly, melted and sieved, to glaze

Line tartlet tins with the pastry (use boat-shaped tins if you have them). Bake blind in a preheated oven at 190°C/375°F/Gas 5 for about 10 minutes. When cold, brush the insides of the tartlet cases with the melted chocolate and leave to harden.

Mix together the cream cheese and double cream until very smooth, then add the sugar and vanilla essence. Fill the tartlet cases with the cream mixture and place fruit on top. Brush with apricot or redcurrant glaze, depending on the fruit used, and leave to set.

JP

Raspberry Shortcake

This is not shortcake in the Scottish sense but more the American variety which is really like a sponge cake that soaks up all the juices from the berries. Good and gooey, a delight to all children and grown-ups alike.

350g/12oz fresh raspberries or frozen raspberries slowly thawed
200g/7oz self-raising flour
25g/1oz ground almonds
¼ tsp salt
½ tsp cinnamon
85g/3oz butter, softened
85g/3oz caster sugar
1 egg, beaten
150ml/¼ pint milk
1 tbsp raspberry jam
25g/1oz icing sugar
¼ pint double cream

Sift flour, almonds, salt and cinnamon into a bowl and rub in the butter, mix in the sugar. Add the beaten egg and milk to make a scone-like dough. Divide dough in two and gently shape each half to fit into greased 20cm/8in sandwich tins. Cook in a preheated oven at 230°C/450°F/Gas 8 for 10–15 minutes. Remove from the oven and cool on a wire rack. When cold spread one of the layers with raspberry jam, then generously with the double cream and raspberries. Sprinkle raspberries with icing sugar, cover with the second layer and top with more cream. Decorate with a few raspberries. Best eaten when fresh.

JP

Illustrated overleaf

233

Peaches Cardinal Hume

This is one of the best ways of eating peaches. An old receipt, I have added Hume to the Cardinale because the saintly man lives round the corner from me and I often have chats with him from my motor-bike and I love him.

10 ripe large peaches
450g/1lb granulated sugar
1.4 litres/2½ pints water
1 vanilla pod
450g/1lb raspberries
200g/7oz caster sugar

Put the granulated sugar into a saucepan large enough to hold the peaches. Add the water and the vanilla pod and bring to the boil, gently to begin with, stirring until the sugar dissolves. When simmering put in the peaches. Bring back to simmering point and very gently poach for 8 minutes. Remove the peaches and peel while still warm. The syrup can be bottled and used to poach other fruits. Put the peaches into a beautiful glass dish and chill.

Liquidise the raspberries with the caster sugar and pass through a sieve if you wish to get rid of the pips. When ready to eat, pour the glorious red purée over the succulent peaches. Decorate with mint leaves dragged through icing sugar.

JP

Cherries Jubilee

Bulgaria produces some first-rate tinned cherries if you can find them, or if they are
in season you can use fresh ones stewed in syrup.

450g/1lb tin stoned black
cherries
grated rind of 1 lemon
55g/2oz caster sugar
a good pinch of ground
cinnamon
3 tbsp Kirsch or similar liqueur
1 dessertspoon cornflour
3 tbsp granulated sugar
125ml/4floz cognac

Drain the cherries but reserve the juice. Mix the fruit with the lemon rind, caster sugar, cinnamon and liqueur and leave to steep until needed, at least 2 hours – the longer the better. Ice cream is served with these cherries, so buy or make the best vanilla you can.

When you are about to eat this pudding, blend the cornflour with the steeping juices from the cherries until quite smooth. Add a few spoons of the tinned juice. Pour into a frying pan and stir over a low heat until clear and thickened. Pour in more tinned cherry juice if necessary. Stir in the cherries to heat through. Sprinkle with the granulated sugar, add the cognac and then set fire to the whole mixture, spooning the juices over and over until the flames abate. Serve poured over the ice cream. Very luscious.

JP

Coconut Blancmange with Cranberry Sauce

A pale and interesting pudding with a dramatic red sauce. Even those who dread the word blancmange will like the coconut effect, I hope. My various sojourns in the West Indies have left me with a taste for the fruit and a large supply of recipes.

350g/12oz desiccated coconut
1.2 litres/2 pints milk
6 tbsp cornflour
115g/4oz caster sugar
115g/4oz cranberries
55g/2oz sugar
juice of ½ a lemon

Put the coconut and milk in a saucepan and heat to a simmering point. Remove from the heat and stand for 30 minutes for the flavour to infuse. Strain through a cheesecloth, pressing to extract all the liquid.

Put the cornflour in a large bowl and blend to a smooth paste with some of the coconut milk. Put the rest of the coconut milk and caster sugar in a pan, heat gently until the sugar dissolves then bring to the boil. Pour quickly over the cornflour, stirring briskly. Return to the heat and stir until large bubbles break the surface. Pour into a wetted mould, cool to room temperature, chill and unmould. Heat the cranberries with the sugar and lemon juice and pour over the blancmange.

CDW

Apricot Shortcakes

The recipe for these good little cakes comes from the late Michael Smith.

MAKES 16–20

150g/6oz plain flour
100g/4oz unsalted butter
50g/2oz ground rice
50g/2oz caster sugar
apricot jam

Sift the flour into a bowl and rub in the butter to the texture of fine breadcrumbs. Add the ground rice and sugar and mix well. Put 40g/1½oz apricot jam in the centre of the mixture and work into a smooth dough.

Roll out to 2cm/¾in thick and cut into shapes. Place on greased baking sheets. With a thimble make a small hollow in the middle of each biscuit and place a little jam in each. Bake in a preheated oven at 180°C/350°F/Gas 4 for 20 minutes. Cool on a wire rack.

CDW

Maids of Honour

How singularly unapt is the name for these little medieval tarts. Henry VIII called them this after Anne Boleyn when she was lady in waiting to Catherine of Aragon. If Anne had only had a little more honour, or perhaps a little less, England might still be Catholic.

MAKES 12

600ml/1 pint fresh milk
1 tsp rennet
pinch of salt
115g/4oz unsalted butter
2 egg yolks
2 tbsp brandy
15g/½oz slivered almonds
1 tsp sugar
1 tsp ground cinnamon
grated rind and juice of ½ lemon
225g/8oz puff pastry
currants to decorate

Warm the milk to blood heat, then add the rennet and salt. Leave the resulting curds to drain in muslin overnight.

Sieve the curds and butter together. Beat the egg yolks briskly with the brandy and add to the curd mixture. Add the almonds, sugar, cinnamon and lemon rind and juice.

Line patty tins with the puff pastry. Fill with the curd mixture and sprinkle with the currants. Bake in a preheated oven at 220°C/425°F/Gas 7 for 20–25 minutes or until well risen and golden brown.

CDW

Almond Pastry (The Snake)

I remember reading somewhere that this recipe originated in Morocco, and that the literal translation of its Moroccan name is 'the snake' This might help to explain the coiling of the pastry. The almond paste mixture also makes delicious petits fours.

225g/8oz ground almonds
225g/8oz icing sugar, sifted, plus more for dusting
2–3 tbsp orange flower water
½ tsp almond essence
1 egg white, stiffly whisked
6 sheets of filo pastry
melted butter

Mix together the ground almonds, icing sugar, orange flower water and almond essence to make a firm, dryish paste. Knead until smooth. Mix half the egg white into the paste; the remaining egg white will not be needed.

Divide the paste into three, and roll each piece into a long sausage shape about 2cm/¾in thick. Take a sheet of filo pastry and brush with melted butter. Cover with another sheet of filo and again brush with melted butter. Arrange a piece of almond paste lengthways on the filo pastry and roll up carefully.

Have ready a greased loose-bottomed 20cm/8in flan tin. Carefully curl the pastry roll into a spiral, or Chelsea bun shape, in the tin, starting in the centre. Make two more long sausage-shaped rolls, joining the second on to the end of the first and the third to the end of the second and coiling round to the side of the tin. Brush 'the snake' well with melted butter, then bake in a preheated oven at 180°C/350°F/Gas 4 for 30 minutes or until golden brown. Cool in the tin on a wire rack. Remove from the tin and dust with icing sugar when cool.

JP

Bread and Butter Pudding

I must admit that I am not fond of this much-loved pudding, but this is a very good way to make it, using stale croissants rather than bread.

2 stale croissants
softened butter
25g/1oz sultanas
85g/3oz sugar
2 eggs
400ml/14floz liquid (half milk and half cream)
grated lemon rind
freshly grated nutmeg

Slice and butter the croissants. Place in a buttered ovenproof dish in layers, sprinkling the sultanas and 55g/2oz of the sugar between the layers. Beat the eggs with the remaining sugar. Bring the milk and cream just to the boil, and pour on to the egg mixture. Mix well together, then strain into a jug and add the grated lemon rind. Pour the custard over the layered croissants and leave to stand for 1 hour before cooking.

Place the dish in a bain-marie containing enough hot water to come half way up the dish. Grate a little nutmeg over the top of the pudding and bake in a preheated oven at 170°C/325°F/Gas 3 for about 45 minutes or until the custard is set.

JP

Zuppa Inglese

This curious Italian name, making you think of soup, is in fact a good old-fashioned English trifle, far removed from the sort of thing you used to get in the nursery. The Italians took it to their hearts and have loved it ever since.

4 egg yolks
4 tbsp sugar
1 tsp vanilla essence
40g/1½oz plain flour, sifted
tiny pinch of salt
600ml/1 pint milk
150ml/¼ pint Marsala
1 sponge cake, sliced crosswise into three layers
85g/3oz chocolate, grated

Put egg yolks in a bowl, gradually add sugar and vanilla essence, cream well, add flour, pinch of salt and 150ml/¼ pint milk. Boil remaining milk, pour on to the mixture in the bowl, stir well and return to the saucepan. Simmer gently, stirring constantly for about 3–4 minutes. Pour a third of the mixture into a bowl, add 55g/2oz of grated chocolate and stir until chocolate has melted. Leave both mixtures to cool.

Place a layer of sponge cake on a serving dish, sprinkle with Marsala and cover with a layer of plain custard. Add another layer of sponge, more Marsala and cover with the chocolate custard. Add the last layer of sponge, sprinkle with Marsala and cover with the remaining plain custard. Sprinkle the remaining chocolate over the custard.

JP

Scones

Fresh scones, still warm from the oven, are part and parcel of the delicious teas of my childhood. No-one seems to make them nowadays, they buy terrible things in supermarkets tasting of bi-carb and studded with soggy fruits. They take but a moment, do try them. The savoury ones are perfect to eat with cocktails and you can make them in miniature.

MAKES ABOUT 12

225g/8oz self-raising flour
a small pinch of salt
55g/2oz butter
150ml/¼ pint milk, fresh or sour

Mix the flour and salt in a large bowl. Rub in the butter with your fingertips until it all resembles crumbs. Mix in the milk. Form into a soft dough with a palette knife. Knead lightly on a floured board, then pat out into a round 2cm/¾in thick. Cut into 5cm/2in rounds with a cutter or a little cup.

Place on a greased and floured baking tray and brush with milk. Bake in preheated oven at 220°C425°F/Gas 7 for 10 minutes until well risen and brown. Cool on a rack but eat when still warm, with lots of butter, clotted cream and jam. Yummo.

VARIATIONS
Sweet scones: Add 55g/2oz caster sugar to the dry ingredients.
Fruit scones: Add 55g/2oz dried fruit and 25g/1oz caster sugar.
Savoury scones: Add 85g/3oz finely grated hard cheese and 1 tsp dry mustard or 55g/2oz chopped olives, anchovies or what you fancy.

JP

Barm Brack

This excellent fruit bread is associated with St Brigid in Ireland and is eaten there on her feast day, the 1st February. In other places it was eaten at Hallowe'en when there was a thimble, button or silver coin lurking inside, or even a gold ring.

20g/¾oz fresh yeast
½ tsp white sugar
1 tbsp tepid water
450g/1lb strong white bread flour
1 tsp salt
½ tsp each ground cinnamon and nutmeg
55g/2oz butter
85g/3oz soft brown sugar
1 egg, beaten
300ml/½ pint tepid milk
115–140g/4–5oz sultanas
55g/2oz finely chopped mixed candied peel
milk and sugar to glaze

Blend the yeast with the white sugar, water and ½ tsp of the flour. It is ready when it becomes frothy.

Sift the remaining flour into a bowl with the salt and spice. Rub in the butter, then add the brown sugar and make a well in the centre. Pour in the creamed yeast, the beaten egg and most of the tepid milk. Mix into a dough and beat until it begins to leave the side of the bowl. Add the fruit and peel. Turn into a warmed, greased loaf tin, cover and leave to rise for an hour or so, until almost double in size.

Preheat the oven to 200°C/400°F/Gas 6. Bake the brack for 10 minutes, then lower the heat to 180°C/350°F/Gas 4 and bake for a further 45 minutes. Paint the top with a little milk and sugar and return to the oven for a few minutes.

JP

Scottish Seed Cake

This is my Aberdonian grandmother's recipe, and is more interesting than the English variety.

450g/1lb butter, at room temperature
450g/1lb caster sugar
9 eggs, beaten
450g/1lb plain flour
½ tsp each ground cinnamon and grated nutmeg
115g/4oz candied citron peel, chopped
55g/2oz each candied orange and lemon peel, chopped
115g/4oz blanched almonds, chopped
25g/1oz caraway comfits

Cream the butter and sugar together well. Beat in the eggs. Sift the flour and spices over the surface and fold into the mixture, together with the candied peel and almonds. Sprinkle the top with the comfits. Turn into a greased and lined 25cm/10in cake tin. Bake in a preheated oven at 180°C/350°F/Gas 4 for 2 hours.

CDW

Walnut and Marmalade Teabread

Marian MacNeill surmised that if every French woman was born with a saucepan in her hand every Scots woman was born with a rolling pin. I remember my Aberdonian grandmother saying she was referring to the Scottish ability to bake, not to deal with husbands when they came home drunk! Certainly when I was young it was the great test of a woman's suitability as a daughter-in-law. There is nothing nicer than the smell of baking through the house and it is one of my objections to microwaves that our children will grow up without the smell of food cooking. This is a very satisfying teabread for a lazy afternoon.

225g/8oz plain flour
pinch of salt
1 tbsp baking powder
115g/4oz butter
55g/2oz caster sugar
55g/2oz chopped walnuts
grated rind of 1 orange
2 eggs, beaten
3 tbsp marmalade
2–3 tbsp milk

Grease and carefully line a 450g/1lb loaf tin. Sift the flour, salt and baking powder into a bowl, rub in butter until the mixture resembles breadcrumbs. Stir in the sugar, nuts and rind. Add the eggs, the marmalade and sufficient milk to make a fairly soft batter. Turn into the loaf tin and bake in a preheated oven at 180°C/350°F/Gas 4 for 1¼–1½ hours or until well risen and golden brown. Turn out and cool on a wire rack.

CDW

Index